Our Struggle to Serve

Our Struggle to Serve

The Stories of 15
Evangelical Women

Virginia Hearn, Editor

WORD BOOKS
PUBLISHER
WACO, TEXAS

OUR STRUGGLE TO SERVE

Copyright © 1979 by Word, Incorporated, Waco, Texas 76703
ISBN 0–8499–0089–1
Library of Congress catalog card number: 78–59434
Printed in the United States of America

Chapter 11 is adapted from "Lost and Found," chapter 16, in *Alone: A Widow's Search for Joy* by Katie F. Wiebe. Copyright 1976 by Tyndale House Publishers, Wheaton, Illinois. Used by permission.

Appendix 1, "Woman's Work," by Mildred Meythaler is reprinted by permission from *HIS* (January, 1960), student magazine of Inter-Varsity Christian Fellowship. Copyright 1960.

Appendix 2, "Second-Class Citizenship in the Kingdom of God" by Ruth A. Schmidt, is reprinted from *Christianity Today,* Jan. 1, 1971. Used by permission. Copyright 1971.

In memory of my mother
GLADYS FAIR KRAUSS
1891–1977

Contents

Preface

CURRER BELL AND George Eliot were seemingly male pseudonyms for two nineteenth-century women now recognized among the world's great novelists. In the late eighteenth century, a powerful writer was described by some who had not read her book, which is still in print in the 1970s, as a "hyena in petticoats." (That was Mary Wollstonecraft.) Commenting on the literary output of women over the centuries, Joan Goulianos says: "They wrote in a world that was controlled by men, a world in which women's revelations, if they were anything but conventional, might not be welcomed, might not be recognized—and they wrote nevertheless."

In 1974 an *Eternity* magazine poll chose the first "evangelical feminist" book, *All We're Meant to Be,* as the year's most significant book. Yes, times are different now.

Or are they? In 1975 a Christian newspaper in Berkeley received the greatest reader response in its history to a short autobiographical article on egalitarian marriage—gentle, nonpolemical—by a young Christian married couple. With one exception, response was all negative, all male.

I am indebted to Letha Scanzoni and Nancy Hardesty, authors of *All We're Meant to Be,* and to their publisher, Word Books, for thus paving the way for *Our Struggle to Serve: The Stories of 15 Evangelical Women.* One of my husband's students, Ann Hammon, unknowingly gave me, and the rest of my family, our first insights into the "women's movement" when she lived with us and parked her extensive feminist library on our living room mantel. My sister, Kathryn Long, perseveringly encouraged me toward a writing career during

a period in the '50s when I was a discouraged high-school
teacher. Anne Eggebroten has been a stalwart friend, giving
me the idea for this book and remaining firmly supportive
throughout its long gestation. My husband Walter has loved
me in spite of everything—and taken time to "edit the editor."
My friend and neighbor Bill Colbert typed the manuscript with
alertness and patience, and Linda Duddy did hours of proof-
reading. I am grateful to them all.

VIRGINIA HEARN

Berkeley, California
September 1978

Introduction

Virginia Hearn

Women's Place in the Evangelical Milieu:
Is Progress Possible?

I REMEMBER MY FIRST philosophical discussion. It took place among a group of fifth graders. I don't recall its antecedents, but I have never forgotten the topic: Is it better to be a boy or a girl? To the commendation of my parents—who had three daughters, no sons—*I* was completely satisfied with my lot in life. But I was surprised at the almost total agreement that it was better to be male. A number of girls even said they wished they were boys, but no boys said they would rather be girls. As for me, my reasons were totally superficial: girls have prettier clothes; men have to do harder and dirtier work. Such was my ten-year-old naiveté.

In retrospect, it seems to me that my parents did not lay "feminine" role expectations on my sisters and me in our early years. My mother, for instance, refused to let me join a 4-H club, even though 4-H taught very young girls to cook and sew. (She thought 4-H mothers ended up doing most of the work.) That each of us would get a good education and have a career was taken for granted. Perhaps such goals have frequently characterized the outlook of families where one or

---

Virginia Hearn has been an editor for twelve years, with HIS *magazine, InterVarsity Press, the Christian Medical Society; most recently as a free-lancer for various Christian publishers and Holt, Rinehart and Winston. She and her husband Walter work as an editorial team in Berkeley, California. Her first book was* What They Did Right: Reflections on Parents by Their Children.

both parents was an immigrant. Always there was the theme
in our home that we would "have it better" than our parents,
and basic to that improvement was education.

My father had come with his parents to the United States
from Germany early in this century. Education beyond country
school was impossible for him, but after World War I he left
his father's farm, got a town job working in a laundry, and
eventually bought the laundry. Both my parents were hardworking, frugal, self-sacrificing, and sensitive—and to my sisters
and me, that was our primary model for what being grownup
meant in both sexes. For several summers before I reached
my teens, I went down to my father's laundry in the mornings
and worked with three other women on a mangle. I was proud
to do it, in spite of the soaring heat and high humidity of summer in southern Wisconsin. I was glad to earn a quarter for
my three hours' work. My mother went there afternoons.

In a small town like the one I grew up in, we had few visible
models for womanhood. There were schoolteachers (all single
or widowed), librarians, nurses, clerks in stores, waitresses, and
those hardworking women in my father's laundry. A very few
women, like the mothers of some of our friends, had time to
lie in the sun, smoke, drink, and play golf. Such mothers also
let their children buy too much candy and pop, read comic
books, and go to the movies every Saturday afternoon. My
mother regarded those women with outspoken abhorrence—
so such a model for adult female life was out of the question
for my sisters and me.

My own home would hardly have been called traditional,
though my mother was diligently fulfilling many of the usual
female roles. My father was the breadwinner, which he regarded as entitling him to be the family's decision-maker. He
did all the grocery shopping on Saturday mornings. He chose
what to buy, though my mother occasionally gave him a short
list. He told her each morning what to serve for meals that
day. At suppertime and on Sundays he helped with the cooking—frying potatoes, superintending the meat, etc. He made
all home-decorating decisions—paint color, wallpaper, furniture—often against the preference of everyone else. It was
he who took my sisters and me as children to shop for our
store-bought clothes. Likewise, the choices were his when my

mother needed a new coat, dress, or even a hat. She submitted to it all, never questioning his right to such patriarchal authority. By the time I was eleven or twelve, however, I was already becoming a crusader for "justice"; I started to challenge his monolithic control. A predictable result of my father's dominance was my sisters' and my secretiveness, a conscious or unconscious decision to keep things to ourselves ("What he doesn't know won't hurt him"—or us). Rather than being defiant or malicious, it was a kind of self-defense.

With the advent of "mixers" after school in junior high, and after-game dances and proms in high school, the pervasive male-female hierarchy of the sexist society in a small midwestern town was undeniable: always the boys got to choose; the girls waited along the wall, or danced with one another. A voracious reader, I picked up the term *wallflower* at an early age—and oh, how desperately I didn't want to be that: a wallflower. A *drip*. But by then the expectations of my parents had subtly changed—or I should say, increased. Academic and musical success was Number One, but close to it was popularity. Boyfriends. I read all the books in the library on how to succeed, I had neat hair and clean fingernails, but I was also outspoken and competitive and plump. In junior high I encountered a new word—*flirt* (it was something girls did)—and I recall discussing with a friend what it meant. She and I never learned. Our most earnest longing during those years was to get away from it all and go to a girls' boarding school, where they *all* had such fun, and where there were no boys! To my parents such a possibility was unimaginable.

When I was nineteen and in college, I became a Christian through a dorm Bible study. Suddenly I was immersed, at least on Sundays, in the evangelical milieu. I went with a girlfriend (who had led the Bible study) to a house church in Columbus, Ohio, a tiny group of the breed called Plymouth Brethren. The "sistern" wore hats, had long hair, and sat in silence through two long services. The format was somewhat like a Quaker meeting, except it was biblically-oriented. The Spirit moved only the men to speak.

There was a small Christian group called Life Work Recruits on what was otherwise a very liberal, though church-related,

campus. That group consisted largely of kids from fundamentalist churches. To have someone from a different background,
from out-of-state, become a Christian there and be more or
less active among them was unusual. I never felt liked or
accepted.

I have no doubt that Inter-Varsity Christian Fellowship preserved me for the Christian faith. I read I-V books, subscribed
to *HIS* magazine, and went to I-V conferences—where women
did speak, although they never served at the occasional communion services. I took the kind of Christian commitment that
Inter-Varsity stood for with immense seriousness. (Eventually,
having a kind of literary bent, and by the grace of God, I
became assistant editor of the Inter-Varsity magazine. At that
time, I moved to the cold and closed eastern society of Philadelphia, where even Christianity hadn't done much to warm up
the evangelical milieu.)

High school had taught me that a girl who was conspicuously
intelligent—unless she was also very beautiful, a "swan"—had
a hard time of it. So during my college years I deliberately
shut my mouth in classes. I stopped risking myself in the male-
dominated world of spoken words and debate. All that counted,
I reasoned, was performance on tests—and no one else had
to know how you did. That way you won the respect of professors, you got good grades, yet you didn't have three strikes
against you socially.

My silence in class reflected a psychological state that has
recently been described as the "motive to avoid success." The
"dominant societal stereotype views competence, independence, competition, and intellectual achievement as qualities
basically inconsistent with femininity, even though positively
related to masculinity and mental health. . . . [Therefore] a
girl who maintains the qualities of independence and active
striving necessary for intellectual mastery defies the conventions of sex-appropriate behavior and must pay a price in
anxiety. . . . In the later college years girls experience a sud-
den reversal in what parents applaud for them; i.e., whereas
they have previously been applauded for academic success
these girls now find themselves being evaluated 'in terms of
some abstract standard of femininity with an emphasis on marriage as the appropriate goal for girls of this age.' " [1]

When I became a Christian I also became more concerned about my image, my "witness." In one sense, I became less self-confident. The Bible seemed to reinforce this: The man "was not deceived," it said, "but the woman was deceived . . ." (1 Tim. 2:14).[2] I lost a good bit of social confidence by being a woman per se. College students, in those years, were called the Silent Generation. And as with many other issues of the fifties—racism, for example—I passively accepted my second-class role as a Christian woman as *the way it was.* I had no vision for the possibility of things being otherwise.

After college, such a role was bearable largely because with *HIS* magazine in Philadelphia I had a meaningful job. I believed that I was serving God; I believed that what I was doing, editing articles and so on, was helping people in their Christian lives. And that was all that counted in the long run.

One characteristic of the evangelical world in the field of journalism was this: A woman could hold a significant job and do much of the interesting work, even though a man's name was invariably on the masthead of the magazine above hers. There was too much prejudice against a woman's "having authority over men" or "teaching men" for it to be otherwise.

I have hesitated to write on this topic because my experience as a woman in the evangelical milieu has been somewhat negative. But here let me point to an indication of progress. After I had worked for two years with *HIS,* the editor resigned. Who would succeed him? Never would I have aspired to that position, yet the editor told me that he was recommending me as one possibility for his successor. He added, however: "But I don't think they will appoint a woman as editor." They didn't. That was 1959. Now, not quite twenty years later, *HIS* magazine does have a woman editor: Linda Doll, who worked on Inter-Varsity staff in New England for many years.

So . . . things change. There *has* been progress for women in the evangelical world, at least in journalism. And, before that development with *HIS,* there was Sharon Gallagher, who since 1973 has been editor of *Radix,* newspaper of the Berkeley Christian Coalition. And there is Bonnie Greene in Toronto, a wife and mother, who until recently edited *Vanguard* for those Reformationists up there—men and women who take Scripture as seriously as anybody.

Nevertheless, in Philadelphia it was discouraging to be a single woman in evangelical circles. I attended a church out in the remote suburbs, where the expository preaching was excellent. But it was clearly a couples' church, a family church. I can think of only one other single woman there at the time. She was older and better known; she taught in the Christian school where many of their children went. There was no place for me in that church, which was so obvious that I was never even invited to the women's meetings. Like Ralph Ellison, who wrote about being a black person in the U.S. in the twenties and thirties and forties, I was an "Invisible Person." Oh, some people spoke to me each Sunday—but that I had a life outside those church doors, or would welcome human contact, apparently went unsuspected by almost everyone. There was a good-looking young single man in that church, an engineer, and he seemingly had lots of dinner invitations. One couple did invite me over—because they wanted me to "be a witness" to the husband's younger sister, who was also always invited.

I was very poor in those days, as people in Christian work still often are, and I didn't have a car. That church was almost out in the country, quite a ways from the trolley line and the city bus service. You got there by taking an intercity bus that would stop and let you off near the church driveway and then you caught it again by waiting out on the highway until it came along and you flagged it down. Church people drove by me there on the highway after the service, occasionally waving, usually not even recognizing me. As I said, I was invisible. (Eventually, some college-age kids began attending that church and, in my final months in Philadelphia, gave me a ride both ways.)

Has the situation improved today in evangelical churches? Most of my single friends say not; there seems to be no place for them. And what the solution to that problem is, I don't know. My husband and I do seem to have more single people in our home than married couples. That may be from conscious recognition of their need or from unconscious recognition that we have more in common with them. What seems clear is that single people need both single and married friends, good friends, and vice versa.

As I have continued in the field of journalism and editing,

and as my consciousness has been raised, I have become increasingly aware of the pervasive use of the generic in Christian writing (using *he, him, mankind,* though both sexes are meant). For as long as I can remember, I have been sensitive to language, to words. As a seventh grader, when the generic was first explained in our English class, I was troubled by it. Why should something be stated in a male way, yet claim to include me when it clearly didn't? The generic makes women, sisters, and daughters invisible—we are subsumed under a male entity that doesn't fit us. Translators of the Bible over the centuries, acculturated by their own milieu, have been among the worst offenders. In several instances when the original Greek of the New Testament used the word for human beings in general, without any sexual designation, the English translation became "men," "brothers," or "sons." And there is the appalling example of a particular Greek word being translated "deacon" when a man was meant, but translated "servant" when referring to a woman (Phoebe, in Rom. 16:1, KJV).

Recently I discovered one male writer who was willing to admit that such language "is *functionally* sexist and therefore ought to be replaced as much as possible. . . . For me, as a male, the word *man* can be used either generically or particularly and I have no great shift to make in my consciousness: I know instantly that I am included. . . . For a woman it requires a deliberate shift in consciousness to sense herself included in the word *man*. . . . It would be insensitive and un-Christian for males to insist on using male references for generic terms when they cause pain to women and no longer communicate as intended. The way of Christ is the way of love, care, and understanding; it is not the way of coercion and insensitivity." [3]

As for progress at that level among evangelical book publishers, I know there has been some—specifically among the ones my husband and I work for as editors. It is almost always possible for us to add *and women,* or to substitute the words *person, individual,* or *human being* (or to pluralize a concept from *he* into *they),* and thus avoid using that insufficient generic. [4]

I am thankful to have a husband who agrees with me on such matters, and I have great pity for married women who don't. For most of our married life, my husband and I have been moving toward a shared-role marriage. Such a marriage "alleviates one of the major grievances of men (sole responsibility for the provider role) and of women (exclusive responsibility for housework and child care). . . . Role sharing is not role reversal." [5] My husband and I try to do things together. Professionally we have become a writing-editing team in which we both "carry our weight." We have a new sense of how God has molded us to supplement and complement one another in our creative work. We are each learning new skills. We have had to grow beyond the role expectations of both sexes that we learned from the culture in which we grew up. For example, I am more conscious of our car's mental and physical health than is my husband. But I find it hard to relate to young children, whereas he, a "nurturant" personality, has been "Uncle Walt" to countless kids. And as a chemist used to working around laboratory sinks, he has more explicit ideas about order in the kitchen than I have. In our life together, we each "win some, lose some."

As a Christian and a wife, I had years to learn the "servant" role, and in some deeply rooted psychological sense I invariably felt guilty if my husband used his time on some household chore that I could be doing instead. I felt I should always be the interruptible one. That was the traditional wifely ideal, but the result was that I had little time for myself or for intellectual activity. Such an outlook eventually breeds resentment. Now, I am gradually learning to avoid what has been called the compassion trap: "women's personal acculturation to the ideal of constant helpfulness. . . . In a situation which demands full exercise of the compassionate mandate, women are much more ready to push aside a creative enterprise in its favor, even though in the long run the latter might well have represented a social contribution of more lasting value. The model for this sort of commitment to essential mundane needs was set by Martha in the New Testament, who chose to exercise her homemaking skills in a hospitable enterprise in preference to listening to divine wisdom." [6] Jesus did not commend her for that. He said that Mary had chosen what was best (Luke 10:42).

"Through love be servants of one another" (Gal. 5:13, RSV). As both my husband's and my consciousness has been raised, as we have understood that our commitment is to "human liberation" and to "justice and equality between the sexes," I have become freer and my husband in some ways has become more of a servant. When the phone rings, and we are both at our desks at home, I am not always the one who gets up to answer it. When mealtimes approach, I am not always the one who takes action. When some errand is to be run, either one of us may do it. My husband has been willing to make some personal professional sacrifice in order to give me more creative opportunities. We both agree that it is better this way. So often, when a choice has to be made between family responsibilities and more professional prestige for the husband, the wife and children end up as losers.

Is there any basis in the Bible for a shared-role marriage? One Christian author who specializes in sociology writes: "Such a pattern for family life isn't contrary to Biblical principles. . . . The most positive examples of marriage in Scripture are those characterized by interdependence, reciprocity, and mutual responsibilities in family matters, spiritual life, and bread-winning. Priscilla and Aquila were co-workers both in earning a livelihood and in Christian ministry; each was capable of working and serving in the same way as the other. And there's good reason to believe that their common interests strengthened their overall marital relationship (Acts 18; Romans 16:3–5; 1 Corinthians 16:19). The couple described in Proverbs 31:10–31 likewise had a [strong] relationship—not in spite of, but quite likely because of the wife's freedom to use her intellectual and business talents outside the home as well as within it. . . . At creation both male and female were assigned the dual responsibility of the family and creative work in the world at large. The gender-linked division of labor which assigns home responsibilities to wives and provider responsibilities to husbands can cut husbands out of family life just as it cuts wives out of occupational life." [7]

Every Christian woman who reveals that she is even slightly "feminist" [8] in her thinking is accustomed to one speedy response: "But what about headship?" What does the Bible mean when it calls the husband the head of the wife? It is immediately obvious what headship does *not* mean. The husband is not the one who makes all decisions. He does not even make all important decisions—importance is often an *a posteriori* in-sight. No, headship does not lie first of all in the area of the brain or intellect (in Bible times, in fact, both thoughts and emotions were imagined to originate in the heart). The biblical metaphor of headship, like the biblical metaphor of being "in Christ," seems to be a spiritual, even mystical analogy: The husband is to represent Christ, the source of life. That is, the husband is to set the tone of Christlikeness in the family. Rather than focusing on his dominance as being at the top of the body (the family), he is called to love his wife and children self-sacrificially, giving them a firsthand example of Christ's love for each of them. He willingly gives them time and atten-tion. He teaches, serves, provides, disciplines. He heals. He is patient, kind, unselfish, and all the other virtues of 1 Corinthi-ans 13. If necessary, he lays down his life for them. To love like Christ is his most important role as husband and father (Eph. 5:25). Of course, those goals are not unlike my goals as a wife—yet I recognize their worth and profound spiritual im-pact all the more when I see them lived out by my husband. Thus I have no problem with the biblical metaphor of headship as I now see it exemplified in our home. On the other hand, I did have problems with the dictatorial view of headship that characterized my parental home. And such a male role is just as offensive to me today as I see it exhibited in some Christian families. It is clear which concept of headship is compatible with the teaching of Christ and with the overall thrust of the apostle Paul.

In putting together this book of "biblical feminist" autobiog-raphies—though not all the writers would describe themselves as such—I wrote to twenty-five representative women, includ-ing some whose names are known nationally through the Evan-gelical Women's Caucus.[9] When I asked each of them to contribute her own story as a chapter, I encountered an incredi-ble amount of fear, uncertainty about personal identity, and inability to get something down in black and white. Here are some of the responses I received from women "out there" in today's evangelical milieu:

—I'm in a time of personal emotional transition in which I have found it very hard to set down thoughts about my life.

—It would be hard for me to write vividly and concretely and yet skirt basic incidents which I am not free to tell.

—I have found it emotionally a great strain to "re-live" so much and so many relationships. The pain has been acute and dredging it all up again tugs at newly developed spiritual solidity.

—I have written a great deal on this subject, but have laid low for a while because of backlash. I could show you a sheaf of letters I have received in response, from both men and women. The price of progress is not without pain.

—I find myself in a new environment, and it is the most conservative theologically I have ever lived in. Ministry with women is opening up to me on all sides . . . but the whole Woman Question is a very hot potato here and I have to walk warily in this area if many doors are not to be shut in my face. . . . I feel I can be used to introduce new ideas and honest thinking if first I become accepted in less controversial areas.

—I am recently divorced. While my interest in feminism was not a causative factor in my divorce, still it was related, and I have this fear that other people relate the two more than was actually the case, and that those who are looking for faults in feminism will be quick to point that out.

—I'm not sure I'd want you to read it: I wouldn't want to depress you. . . . It was so demoralizing, simply terrible, to work on it. . . . I have to live out my life in a certain sphere of society, and I'm not courageous enough to fight by myself, especially when it means fighting my husband and sons. Every week we have to fight through some new battle. In a way these fights are progress; we come to new understandings. . . . But if I were to publish such a chapter, I'd be standing alone in a church of 2,000 people. Even in the most liberal evangelical church, like ours, the hatred and fear of the women's liberation movement is unbelievable. We're so trapped in what we've been taught. The men and women alike are afraid of new social roles. They caricature the women's movement and ridicule it. If I were identified as a feminist, I would never have a chance to speak. . . . You and I will never experience the fruits of this movement; we are only emerging "persons." It will be better for our granddaughters, when it's accomplished, but now it's only a start.

Such responses reveal how much progress still is needed before Christian women can recover the sense of self-worth inher-
ent in being made "in God's image." Is progress possible for
women in today's evangelical milieu? My own life—and the
lives of the courageous women who tell their stories in this
book—show that it is.

NOTES

1. Matina S. Horner, "Toward an Understanding of Achievement-Related
Conflicts in Women," *Journal of Social Issues* 28, no. 2 (1972).

2. Whatever this statement meant—and I take it literally—I am sure that
the divine intent was not to undermine all women's sense of self-worth for
the rest of human history.

3. David Gill, "Prolegomena to the Male/Female Discussion," *Radix*, May
1976.

4. A sophisticated analysis of the language used both by and about women
appears in Robin Lakoff's *Language and Woman's Place* (New York: Harper
& Row, 1975). Lakoff's work is a landmark study in a new area of sociolinguistics
of immense significance for Christians concerned with male-female questions.

5. Jessie Bernard, *The Future of Marriage* (New York: World Publishing
Company, 1972).

6. Margaret Adams, "The Compassion Trap," in *Women in Sexist Society:
Studies in Power and Powerlessness,* ed. Vivian Gornick and Barbara K. Moran
(New York: Basic Books, Inc., 1971).

7. Letha Scanzoni, "Feminism and the Family," *Daughters of Sarah* 1, no.
4 (May 1975).

8. Feminist = advocating legal and social changes to establish the political,
economic, and social equality of the sexes.

9. See Appendix 4. I did not necessarily seek all the "stars" of the evangelical
women's movement or even well-known women. Rather I wanted autobiogra-
phies typical of a widely occurring phenomenon in the evangelical church
today: women finding new personal dimensions of Christ's liberation. Interest
in the celebrity stories that flood the religious publishing market, and sell
hundreds of thousands of copies, seems to stem more from carnal curiosity
than from spiritually motivated response. The lives of ordinary Christians are
more relevant to most of us—and often more compelling as well.

Our Struggle to Serve

Chapter One

Lareta Halteman
Finger

WHAT DOES A mother do with a daughter who begs to "let me just finish the chapter" whenever there are jobs to be done around the house? who never notices housework to begin with? who runs barefoot and climbs trees all summer? who hates to dress up and vows never to wear high heels? whose only interest in the culinary arts consists of turning over pancakes and licking the frosting bowl?

I was that daughter.

I arrived in time to celebrate Christmas 1940, and it was lucky for me, my mother declared later, that I wasn't delivered in a hospital or she would have thought the babies had gotten mixed up in the nursery. Not able to fall back on that explanation, Mom concluded I was like my father in all the wrong ways. It was fine for him to remain ignorant of the art of housekeeping, but for her oldest daughter . . .

My father would smile with just a shade of smugness and declare he'd gotten the right baby after all. Dad was an individual—not one of those "rugged individualists" who take on the world alone, but a true original thinker. Never schooled beyond

---

Lareta Halteman Finger lives in Chicago and is editorial coordinator for Daughters of Sarah. *She, her husband Tom, and two sons are intentional neighbors to a Christian community called Austin Community Fellowship.*

eighth grade, he educated himself in areas of his interest: theology, science, history. Oblivious of powerful forces in society to conform, he pondered over issues alone and came out at different places from his contemporaries. For example, through the late forties and until 1954, when it was fashionable to buy a new car every year or two, he kept our '34 Plymouth in shape for over 100,000 miles. And at a time and place when higher education was looked on askance, my father, with his great joy of learning, wanted all of his five children to experience it to the full—through high school, college, and further, if we wanted.

My father's values became mine. An open mind, a passion for reading and thinking, the importance of the life of the spirit, and an impish desire to flout silly conventions. From this grew a thirst to find out who I was and to live a life that was truly my own.

From my mother I learned to express my emotions. She loved life and she hated life. She was exhilarated at the thought of picking, shelling, and freezing 20 quarts of lima beans in one day. (I understood the emotion but not the reason for it.) She would agonize over what to cook for supper, be ready to sell the lot of us kids down the river, and lament her departure from spinsterhood. (I understood both the emotion and the reason for it.) She would invite the neighbors up for coffee, and their roars of laughter could be heard all over the house. She wouldn't for the world have missed helping us color Easter eggs or wrap Christmas gifts.

Neither of my parents was a strict disciplinarian, and they both had an instinct for giving children space to be themselves. As a consequence, I never learned much about housework but early acquired an independence of spirit that helped me over some rough going later.

I read with a passion. The Bobbsey Twins soon gave way to Nancy Drew, the Hardy Boys, and those small orange volumes describing the childhood of great men and women. Missionary books had immense appeal to me. I dreamed of a future in China like *The Small Woman*. I worked up equal fervor with *Borden of Yale '09*. After hearing one emotional minister describe how Indians in northern Canada were desperate for schoolteachers, my future was certain. I would teach those Indians and help convert them to Christianity. I would lay down my life for the sake of others.

Had I been a boy, the daydreams of my later childhood and emerging adolescence might have merged into reality with less trauma. A man could do all those noble things and still have a wife to cook for him, clean his house, and raise his children. A woman could not. The only way a woman could achieve greatness and truly serve God and other people was by foregoing her natural desires. I decided never to get married.

I came from Swiss-German stock, Mennonites living quietly and growing wealthy in rural southeastern Pennsylvania. Over the centuries they had developed a subculture all their own. During my early years, momentum was gathering, for better and worse, for greater assimilation into broader American society.

Everything in my culture was geared toward marriage. It was a necessity because of the rigid sex roles played out by the people of my community. A man worked on the farm or in business. He needed a wife to manage the house and raise his children. Women found their identity being someone's wife and someone else's mother—and discussing it all in the church basement Sunday morning when the children could no longer sit quietly through the sermon.

My culture was loading me with double messages. Mennonites had an early history of radical nonconformism and leadership for both men and women. They had taken initiative in foreign missions and relief work. But that was all theory to me: the vivid pictures I pored over in *Martyrs' Mirror,* the maps in Sunday school showing where our missionaries were working. What I actually *saw* were men and women acting out staid, traditional roles. If godliness came first, cleanliness and the status quo ran a close second.

As I saw them, women fell into three categories: wives who stayed at home and raised children, older single women who had neither family nor career, and schoolteachers. I had a number of single female teachers at our Mennonite school; all of them either remained single or quit teaching or moved away when they married. My experience echoed Betty Friedan's, who wrote that she never knew a woman, when she was growing up, who used her mind in an intellectual way, played her own part in the world, and also loved and had children (*The Feminine Mystique*, W. W. Norton & Co., Inc., N.Y., 1963, p. 75).

When I began announcing my great plans for celibacy and missionary work, no one took me seriously. "Just wait till you meet Mr. Right." "When you fall, you'll fall hard." When I persisted, religious logic was used: "If you stay single, you'll become ingrown and selfish. A woman needs a husband, and especially children, to get her out of herself and to learn to give. Marriage is God's best plan for women."

To my childish mind this philosophy sounded dead wrong. Was marrying and settling down in rural Pennsylvania an unselfish act? Having children of one's own sounded like a deliberate escape from involvement in the suffering and needs in other parts of the world. It struck me as one of the most selfish choices a woman could make. But I found not a soul who agreed with me.

It is hard to be a nonconformist teen-ager. But teen-age nonconformity in the fifties was even harder—family-oriented and quasi-religious as that decade turned out to be. I overreacted from gut-level feelings and would have scarcely anything to do with boys. To me, boys meant dating, dating meant going steady, falling in love, engagement, marriage, and the harried housewife trap I was avoiding.

Fortunately, I had no trouble relating to girls, women, or older men. I attended the local Mennonite high school and loved it. At that age, the boys in my class generally lagged behind the girls in leadership and maturity, so I had many opportunities for expressing myself. I secretly enjoyed my notoriety, looked down on the boys, and—had the name then been invented—would have been called a reverse sexist. No wonder teaching about women's submission to men made no sense to me.

At sixteen, my first opportunity for a date presented itself. A boy several years older than I, whom I did not know very well, asked to take me home from a meeting one evening. I turned him down and drove home in a cold sweat, cursing my entry into the adult world. All of society's pressure toward marriage had made me scared to death of boys my own age.

Writing this autobiography has forced me to seek an explanation for adolescent behavior I later became ashamed of. I would like to use the analogy of other, more normal teen-age rebellions. Immature thinking often "throws the baby out with the bathwater"—*e.g.*, some people reject Christianity because of hypocrites in the church, some kids rebel against all authority because of overstern or narrow parents, some students refuse to learn to read because a certain teacher killed all enthusiasm. Even as these reactions occurred in many other young people, I now realize a parallel in my own life.

I didn't fit into any of these categories. School was my bag. I knew nothing of the sullen withdrawal from adult society which so many adolescents experience. I could always talk to my parents. I formed lasting friendships with some of my high school teachers. Already as a teen-ager I had discovered the joy of loving and being loved by a personal Jesus, instead of squirming under the bondage of religious legalism like so many of my peers. But rigid sex stereotypes and expectations I could not stomach. So, out of fear of losing the intellectual, mystical, and spiritual parts of my inner self, I denied my human, female sexuality.

It was a relief to discover what I was doing. For many years I had felt an undercurrent of blind rage in my otherwise fairly contented life. During my teens and twenties I had no vocabulary to describe sex stereotyping, no concepts to explain the frustration of being expected to act in a certain way because I was a woman. I didn't know that a woman could be a total female, relate intimately to a man, and still be a complete person in herself. Everyone thought I was a man-hater—but I always denied it. I now see that I was resisting having my sexual role the top priority in my life.

I did have one relationship with a boy in high school that I truly enjoyed—or would have, without outside interference and my own overreactions. He was new in our senior class and we discovered we had three things in common: a love of nature, a love of learning, and no thought of marriage. We were developing a genuine friendship until I felt pressures from others who looked at it in a more romantic light. My

fear of getting too involved won out, and later I deeply regretted the loss of that friend. I hated myself for not knowing
how to handle the situation.

I continued to pay a high price for my rebellion. During
my four years at Eastern Mennonite College, I observed that
young men were more intelligent and capable than I had realized before. But my pattern of coldness toward men my own
age prevented me from establishing warm and easy friendships
with them. I suffered through some dates, always irritated by
being the "pickee" rather than the "picker," who was often
someone I barely knew. Why couldn't I be allowed to choose
someone I wanted to spend an evening with?

Those years in college could have been so much more fruitful
had I known what I know now about "women's liberation"
and had society's consciousness been raised as it is now. Even
then, at twenty-one, I felt that truly to do my own thing and
become a complete person meant giving up the normal life
that other women lived. Marriage still looked suspiciously like
submission, and housework was basically the woman's job.

After graduation I was asked to serve as dean of girls at
the high school next door to my alma mater. In many ways
this fulfilled my desire for wholeness. I lived in the dorm with
the out-of-state girls; yet my closest contacts with the faculty
were men. For the first time I formed friendships with men
and felt another part of me begin to come alive. These men
respected me as a person and equal. They never put down
my opinions or attributed my mistakes to being "just a woman."

In 1965 I took a year of seminary at Gordon Divinity School
and then went on to get a master's degree in guidance and
counseling at Boston University. Seminary meant more opportunities for friendships with men, but I still felt a deep shyness
and inability to be warm in the way women usually are warm
toward men. I did make some good friends there, and once
fell in and out of love. Four years later, at age twenty-eight,
I married the man I had always considered a good pal in seminary because we had so much in common, spiritually, intellectually and personality-wise. But that is getting ahead of the
story.

My mid- and late-twenties brought on the conflict most career-minded women experience in or before college. I realized

that even though I desired a life of service to others, my needs for companionship and intimate sharing with a husband were also quite strong. I don't know how conscious these needs would have been had there been no one on whom to focus them. But I couldn't forget the depth of spiritual sharing Tom and I had enjoyed. I longed for more of it.

We did get together (luckily it was 1968—leap year!). But it wasn't easy. Without realizing it, I was fighting my old battle of individuality versus sexuality. Coupled with a certain lack of self-confidence, it must have appeared to Tom at times as if I didn't have very much of either. He wasn't perfect either, of course. Now we consider our marriage a triumph of the grace of God working in two incomplete personalities and through a caring, wise Presbyterian church we were attending in the Boston area. We have learned that God wants so much more out of marriage than romance, a nice house, and two lovely children. As our pastor told us in his wedding sermon, "God has used both of you as hammers to mold the other on the anvil of his grace—to forge you into his image." After seven years he continues to do so.

Until 1973 I paid little attention to publicity about the secular women's movement. As a single woman I was too busy already doing what they were talking about: in my jobs of teaching, counseling, and administration. Further, my misconceptions included visions of angry, masculinized women who were not being at all Christian in their ideas of aggressiveness and free love. As a married woman, I hadn't yet fully resolved my old conflict and was unconsciously submerging my spontaneity. I let Tom make the major decisions. It was so much easier, and I thought he was more capable anyhow. As far as I knew, the women's movement hadn't yet penetrated the church. "Biblical feminism" was scarcely a household word.

We spent July '72 to June '73 in Germany while Tom worked on his doctoral dissertation. After a depressing winter of gray skies, constant nausea from early pregnancy, and isolation in a fifth-floor apartment with a one-year-old, spring burst over the land. With it came some new friends, more time in the park, and a greater awareness of myself as a person of worth in God's Kingdom.

That spring I read an article in an American religious periodical written by a woman who was challenging sex-stereotyped occupations. Why was she given a doll for her fourth birthday when she had asked for a tractor? Why didn't more women go into carpentry, plumbing, or medicine? Something clicked inside me.

Then I read some subsequent letters to the editor and nearly exploded. Verses from Paul's and Peter's writings were liberally misquoted to show that a woman's place was irrevocably in the home. Peter called women the weaker sex; therefore any job requiring hard physical labor, such as carpentry, was naturally taboo. Besides, a woman is not truly fulfilled unless she is making a lovely home for her husband and children. "I sew all my husband's pants, and he is so proud of me."

I was off and running. My understanding of the Good News of Jesus Christ was that it liberated women, not consigned them to one narrow box of homemaking. I determined to find out what the New Testament really said. For weeks I labored in a German library where English resources were at a minimum. The result was an article published in the *Gospel Herald,* a Mennonite periodical.

By the fall of '73, after our return to the States, we moved with two very small children to Eastern Mennonite College, where Tom began teaching a heavy load of philosophy. We lived in a tiny apartment for eighteen months. During that time I dealt most intensely with my personal liberation as a woman. I delighted in my children, but many times I felt trapped. I remember the overwhelming feeling of wonder that would come over me holding our children or watching them sleep. On the other hand, the never-ending demands of such little ones can suck discipline and integration out of a woman. There just isn't enough time to spend alone in personal growth. I would read books while sitting on the floor with toys and kids swirling around me. I labored through another article relating to women and housework amid diaper-changing, potty-training, and trips to the laundry.

Tom helped all he could, but he was trapped too—caught in a vise between overwork at school and a desire to relate to his wife and children more fully. Our society seems bent on making a salaried job a man's whole life. Men need liberating too.

The summer of '75, when our boys were nearly two and

four years old, we moved into a large house with another couple, two children, and nine college students. Within this extended family, my feeling of being trapped with the children disappeared. Others helped with our boys and established friendships with them. After they went to sleep in the evening, someone was usually around to listen for them if we wanted to leave. I am also aware, however, that their ages now made a difference. Helping with follow-the-dots or letter recognition appeals to me more than teaching a one-year-old how to eat with a spoon. For some reason I get more of a charge out of Pinnochio or Winnie the Pooh than "see the doggie." I can now foresee a day when I will feel far less conflict between motherhood and personhood.

Throughout this chapter I have been discussing the difficulty I had integrating my sex-related role as wife and mother with my intense desire for completeness. It is easy to condemn American culture for creating this dilemma in women. Sociological treatises like *The Feminine Mystique* or Philip Slater's *The Pursuit of Loneliness* demonstrate clearly the swing to female domesticity after World War II. The feminine "ideal" of a career-minded husband, a nice house in the suburbs, and several children persisted strongly through the fifties and still clings to those who mothered or grew up during those years. I see this pattern as very restrictive to both women and men. Tom and I believe that some type of shared life with the people of God can bring a greater sense of wholeness to both our lives and to our relationship. It can also release more energy and resources for helping others. We are planning to move to Chicago and relate to the Austin Community Fellowship, a group of nineteen Christians who have committed themselves to the Lord and to each other in a special way. We gave Christian community priority over a job. Only after we found this community would Tom accept an offer to teach at a nearby seminary. If he is again bound by too much work, we will do some rethinking with the community. I am also looking forward to getting back into some area of counseling and/or writing.

But external circumstances must be accompanied by internal growth. I could forever resent women's oppression, but if I am not growing toward completeness on the inside, no environmental changes will help.

The spring of '75, while we were still cramped in our apartment, I had an unforgettable experience confronting the enemy that lay within. From childhood on, I had perceived that, for a woman, being loved by a man seemed to be the most important thing in her life. Everything else revolved around that relationship (or later, around the offspring resulting from it). As the poet Byron put it more succinctly: "Man's love is of man's life a thing apart. 'Tis woman's whole existence."

It was this unchallenged premise that I had reacted against so strongly. Yet there I was, home with two babies, and with my husband being my only regular adult relationship. Love in marriage, or the lack of it, indeed seemed my whole existence. We were heavily overloading the circuit. If Tom didn't respond the way I needed him to, there was no other shoulder to cry on. Secretly I had capitulated to that grand illusion.

At the time I was reading some secular literature on women's liberation. My spirits rose to see in actual print some of my own feelings. Contrary to Byron, these writers had some real insight into the subtle ways women are restricted by "love" (that is, domesticity), and allow themselves to remain so.

I was going through a period when I sometimes didn't feel deeply loved by my husband and consequently felt of little worth as a person. Fortunately, things came to a head one evening. I emerged from nameless anxiety and gave myself to utter, cold despair. It was an experience akin to Francis Thompson's in "The Hound of Heaven":

> My harness piece by piece Thou hast hewn from me,
> And smitten me to my knee;
>   I am defenceless utterly.

Along with my feminist literature, I had read an article by Jürgen Moltmann called "The Crucified God." Moltmann emphasizes that God does not stand apart from suffering and try to pull us out of it. Rather, God's love is such that he suffers with us. Jesus' death on the cross demonstrates the willingness of God to enter into humanity's suffering. And not just once, but as long as suffering exists.

Kneeling there, I became aware of the presence of Jesus, not aloof and transcendent but suffering with me, taking my pain into his own spirit. And in the intimacy of shared suffering,

I knew how deeply and irrevocably I was loved. Jesus, the friend of women, had affirmed me. My wholeness as a person did not depend on my husband. It was never intended to. It came from a crucified God whose name is Love; it came from within myself, and from the whole community of believers. I knew now I could go through anything and survive.

Tom could see that something had happened to me. I had freed him from a guilt-obligation to love me, and in that act I had become more lovable. I was able also to strengthen him in some of the difficulties he was having.

Since then, I have grown in confidence and in enthusiasm for life. It is hard to talk about feeling so greatly loved by God and not have it sound like a platitude heard all one's life. But when I consciously keep this knowledge in mind and make all other desires secondary, a lot of frustration is relieved.

The story is not over. I am not yet the woman I would like to be or that God wants me to be. At times I feel at loose ends vocationally because I don't yet have a fulfilling salaried job. Sometimes I am a poor marriage partner. I am not assertive enough, and that annoys me.

But now I have tools to work with and not blind frustration. I feel less like a square peg in a round hole. The Good News has turned out to be good indeed—even for a woman who has never quite fit society's expectations and stereotypes.

Chapter Two

Joyce Gladwell

AMONG MY EXPECTATIONS as I was growing up in the Carib- bean island of Jamaica were two that I did not question: one was that I would have a career; the other, that I would be exempt from household chores.

My mother was a schoolteacher and expected that her daughters would also fit themselves for a suitable profession. She herself had servants and confidently assumed that we would also. When in my teens I complained that I had not learned to cook, Mama brusquely dismissed my complaint. "Any intelligent woman can read a cookbook," she said.

I grew up in the thirties and forties. My father was head teacher in the elementary school in which my mother was an assistant. Both were unquestioningly Christian, convinced of the value of "education," and ambitious for the social advancement of their children.

We lived in the country, my twin sister, a younger brother, my parents, and I, in the sort of isolation exceeded perhaps only by that of pioneer missionaries in a remote bush station. Indeed, my parents' lives bore many resemblances to that of

---

Joyce Eugenie Nation Gladwell was born in Jamaica, West Indies, and is a graduate of University College, London, England. Author of Brown Face, Big Master *(Inter-Varsity Press, 1969), she has lived in Canada with her husband Graham and three sons since 1969.*

missionaries in an alien culture. In their district they stood for enlightenment, hygiene, and Christian standards in a community of struggling small farmers, ignorant and superstitious. Mama was determined to protect us from the ways of the people around us, chief among these being their sexual laxity.

My sister and I were five years old when our brother was born. Mama was prepared for our question, "How do babies come?" "Mother and father come together in a special way," she replied, "and then God gives the mother a baby which grows inside her until it is time to come out." Later she gave us books about puberty so that we found ourselves more knowledgeable in our early teens than other girls at school.

She taught us to look forward to marriage as a special relationship to be desired and cherished. But for all her wisdom and forethought, her protective zeal led her to negative extremes. When puberty came early, she greeted its onset with open distress; our budding breasts were bandaged so that they would not excite attention, and our lives were even more restricted.

Boys, we learned, were to be distrusted. They were sexual predators even though one of this unworthy number was eventually to be accepted as a desirable mate. Girlfriends were also suspect. Mama required us to have no secrets from her so that she might check on the ideas we heard from our friends. My sister and I were compliant and obedient children, and so we were cut off from the trust and privacy in peer relationships that make for social maturity. Our personal and emotional development was bedeviled by insecurity and ambivalence toward marriage and sexuality.

By contrast, my brother was allowed considerable freedom. We had no illusions about the reason: He was free because our society would be amusedly tolerant of his sexual misadventures. We were limited because my mother, thoroughly realistic about the exactions of her contemporaries, feared both for herself and for us the consequences that even a single moral lapse might bring. My father had no part in the extremes of my mother's anxieties. Reserved and bookish, he nourished other sides of our nature. "You are your father's children," my mother would remark about my sister and me, for we shared his love of reading and found great comfort in his company. But he

was withdrawn and rarely talked with us. We learned what
he thought mainly from his public pronouncements, for he
spoke easily and humorously before an audience and was often
in demand to chair meetings and lead local organizations.

At home my mother placed him on a pedestal as head of
the house, to be served first at meals and to have the last word
in making decisions (this often meant that we chose the auspi-
cious moment to consult him so that his decision matched what
the rest of the family wanted). He rarely exerted his authority,
though the influence of his ordered and principled life was
real enough, and his infrequent word of discipline was immediately effective. His detachment sorely tried my mother, who
was more spirited and practical by nature. She held certain
duties to be in my father's province, and when he neglected
them she fretted and badgered him though she could well
have done them herself. But they were bound strongly to each
other, and the slender threads of disharmony and frustration
were woven into a larger pattern of placid and continuing
affection.

Boarding school at the age of twelve reinforced most of what
we learned at home except in one respect: marriage was depre-
cated. Though set in Jamaica, the school was patterned on an
English girls' school, having a marked academic bias with its
sights on Oxford, Cambridge, and London universities for its
graduates. If a girl failed to rise to the complexities of the
quadratic equation or the subtleties of Browning's "Abt Vo-
gler," the staff might console one another with the comment,
"She's got no sense at all, but she's a nice child. Oh, she'll
get married." The school's version of Bernard Shaw's biting
aphorism might have been "Those who can, achieve. Those
who can't, marry."

Thanks to this bias, as well as to my sense of identification
with my father, I was protected from the fallacy that women
are different mentally from men, let alone inferior. I was confident there was a place for me in the wider world. If I didn't
marry before thirty, I promised myself, I would enter politics.
My sister and I threw all our energies into measuring up to
the school's intellectual and moral standards, but our emotional
and social development continued to lag far behind.

At school, drudgery was someone else's duty. In our colonial,

postslavery society with its vast class differences, that chore
fell to the poor, the illiterate, the uncultivated, and (almost
invariably) the black population. The distance between us and
them was further emphasized by the school rule that "girls
may never speak to the maids."

At home that was not so. We spoke to everyone, seeking
to reduce the social distance between us by personal exchange.
I felt the exclusion of the servants at school as a humiliation,
and though I considered the chances remote that I would become a household drudge, the thought nagged at the edges
of my mind that one day I might stand in relation to others
as the servants did to me: set apart, relegated to undesirable
tasks, cut off from equal interchange.

At nineteen, after a break of four months spent at home, I
returned to the school to teach for three years. My sister was
already in England and I joined her in 1953 at University College, London, to read for B.A. honors in psychology and anthropology. Those were halcyon days. After the responsibilities of
teaching and the strictures of home and boarding school, university life in a new country gave me many freedoms.

I continued to escape the burden of drudgery. The university
housed its more fortunate students in residence halls, where
tokens of formal and elegant life reflected the beginnings of
higher education as a preserve of the leisured classes. The par-
quet floors and Indian rugs were kept polished and cleaned
by household staff. Meals were provided, of which dinner, a
formal affair, was followed for those at the high table by coffee
and conversation in the withdrawing room with the principal,
the bursar, and the matron.

The emphases of boarding school, the spiritual and the intellectual, were still uppermost in our lives. We lived close to
people whose ideas and work were changing the history of
learning. The massive figure of biologist J. B. S. Haldane was
a familiar sight as he entered the college daily by the grimy
passageway from Malet Place. J. B. Rhine visited to lecture
on his experiments in extrasensory perception. Eysenck left
his throne at the Maudsley Hospital week by week to expound
to us the empirical basis of psychological testing.

The findings of others who worked elsewhere were brought
to us with stimulating immediacy by our lecturers. The Pilt-

down hoax came to light just after our physical anthropology
professor had pointed out in a lecture the anomalous features
of the skull that made it difficult to define its position in the
evolutionary tableau. Von Frisch had just completed his labori-
ous study of the language of bees, and Wilder Penfield's work
on the human brain opened up the fascinating possibility that
we might be able to locate and isolate specific functions of
"mind." It was an exciting time and place in which to be a
student.

Religious societies drew a fair proportion of students. The
evangelical Christian unions were spiritually nourished by the
London ministries of John Stott and Martyn Lloyd-Jones, whose
churches were within easy access of our residence. For me it
was a peak time of spiritual growth and commitment.

I fell in love with the president of the college's Christian
Union, a mathematics graduate and an Englishman. But at
the end of my course I returned to Jamaica with our relationship in question. His parents were heartsick at the thought
of our marriage. His mother's final word to me was "Joyce, it
is wrong for you to have a white child. It is wrong for Graham
to have a colored child." Gradually their viewpoint changed,
and after eighteen months as a research assistant in education,
I returned to England to marry Graham.

Marriage defeated me completely. My deepest loss was that
of community. For most of my life I had been part of a busy
throng of peers, sharing interests and activities. Now I was
isolated in a corner of a row of London's semidetached dwelling
houses, unrecognized and anonymous, while my husband's life
with his colleagues continued as before. I tried but could not
recover the London of my university days, close-peopled and
carefree. No longer a student, I had lost my favored place in
society—and as the brown-skinned wife of a white native I
paid the penalty of gate-crashing the domestic stronghold.

Pregnancy began at once and cut off the possibility of my
taking a job. Besides, such was unheard of in Graham's family.
Having hurt them enough already, I was willing to fall in with
their expectations in that regard. I adopted their life style,
set my face to become a keeper at home, and found it intolera-
ble. The effort to cook produced its rueful failures as well as

gradual accomplishments, but it also consumed quantities of time and energy.

I even failed to sweep the floor adequately, if that were possible. At least Graham lashed out angrily at me one day, dismayed no doubt by my lack of household skill and rattled by the pressures from his family. "Even my nine-year-old sister could do it better than you, Joyce."

I donned an apron and scrubbed the front steps in full view of all the neighborhood. It was without question a laudable act of conformity to the housewifely ideal, but in my own eyes I had sunk to the lowest point of humanity. Here I came level with the servants at home whose lot had appalled me in childhood.

There was a poem by George Herbert which we had sung as a hymn at school and I remembered well. It ran:

> All may of Thee partake
> Nothing can be so mean
> Which with his tincture, 'for Thy sake,'
> Will not grow bright and clean.

> A servant with this clause
> Makes drudgery divine;
> Who sweeps a room, as for Thy laws,
> Makes that and the action fine.

With that in mind, I reproached myself for my denigration of drudgery. In time I grew to value menial tasks, the routine of active hands and physical demands, as relief from mental strain and intellectual effort. But that acceptance came only after I had developed an inner assurance that domesticity was not my sole or primary role and had begun to put that conviction into practice.

The birth of my son brought to the surface the hostility to my body and to the role of mothering which I had carried with me from childhood. I had longed for a baby but now I felt I was rejecting him. For his sake as well as my own, I wished that someone else would take him and bring him up— someone like my mother-in-law. She stood at the time as the ideal model of motherhood, to which, to my dismay, I found I could not conform. She viewed my distress with bewilderment: "Why can't you make your home and child your career?"

My own mother had returned to teaching three months after the birth of twins. The school where she taught was a few paces from her home. In the tropical warmth she was able to leave my sister and me asleep on an open verandah, where she could see us, and she returned at intervals to breastfeed us. She had servants and a sister-in-law to help her.

For me, English middle-class evangelical society provided no models for combining early motherhood with an active part in the outside world. I tried the woman's meetings of the Plymouth Brethren, of whom we were members, and turned from them in dissatisfaction. They were for older women—and the repetitive singing of choruses, the homilies, and the prayers served only to bind me deeper in depression. I was wretchedly trapped, shut up with everything I hated and cut off from the stimulating world of ideas to which I had been accustomed.

Then, a sliver of relief broke through my wretchedness. I would read my husband's research papers and, though the subject matter was beyond me, I could sense where the presentation was illogical or unclear and could suggest changes. He valued my criticism, since a paper he had rewritten at my suggestion won commendation for him from the Royal Society. In turn this led to an opportunity for me to begin writing.

Through the evangelical Graduates Fellowship, my husband was in touch with a Christian publisher who had a manuscript that needed to be rewritten. It was the story of Christians who resisted and were martyred under communism in Korea. Translated literally from the Korean, the story had to be restructured for western readers. Did Graham know anyone who would do it? He suggested me. I worked for three years to complete it. During that period we moved several times, lived for a while in Jamaica, and two more children were born to us. I finished the manuscript while I recovered after the birth of our third son.

Then I felt empty. I needed another project to occupy my mind, and I began to write about my childhood in Jamaica. It was an exercise to relieve my loneliness. I imagined I was writing for my English friends and neighbors. I wanted to bring together the severed strands of my experience, my childhood in Jamaica and my present life in England, and to explain myself to those around me. In everyday contacts, there seemed no time or opportunity for self-disclosure. "If they won't listen to me," I reasoned, "they might read about me. A book can be taken up and put down at will."

In two years in Jamaica with household help, while Graham lectured at the University of the West Indies, the first draft was complete. The encouragement of a cousin who had done some writing led me to seek publication.

The second draft was written in England on two mornings a week while Graham worked at home and took our youngest, then three years old, back and forth to play-school. I also had cleaning help half a day a week. Six years from its beginnings, the book was finally published—a paperback of less than 200 pages, but for me a tremendously far-reaching achievement.

Like the Judean donkey in Chesterton's poem, I also "had my hour." The book was well received and sold 25,000 copies in three years. It was given readings on the B.B.C., and I was interviewed on local and national television in England. When we moved to Canada that same year, the book eased our reception into the community where we settled and led to many invitations to speak.

While I was writing the second draft of that book, another process was being worked out. The unresolved conflicts of my childhood and early marriage came to a head in two years of psychotherapy. My initial concern was for our eldest son who had borne the brunt of my unhappiest years. For myself, there was persistent ill-health, spasms of abdominal pain, and cystitis which threatened to become chronic. The process of unraveling and insight restored my health and brought me to an emotional turning point which is the theme of another book, one taking more than six years to complete.

The process of change and development continues, with the difference that I am not working alone. I have recovered "community." It is not only that the larger "women's movement" is bursting around me at a time when my own awareness is keenest, but more particularly I have found community in the small Canadian town where we live. Here small groups for awareness and personal growth led by a Mennonite minister

have given Graham and me the opportunity to learn openness
about feelings and relationship in exchange for the petrifying
tradition of reticence in which we were reared. Coming to
know people intensively in a short time has brought us more
quickly into satisfying friendships than the slow process of social
acquaintance would allow. The practical caring of these people
has made up for the separation from our own relatives.

Other groups have provided activities at a different level.
My concern for housebound wives with young children found
expression in initiating with other mental health volunteers
a group for mothers. While their children are cared for one
morning a week, the women share common interests and activities. Out of this a cooperative nursery school was started. Later
our local government built a day-care center, drawing on the
support of the women and providing room in their building
for a privately run school.

As I grew in self-confidence and found fulfilling opportunities
in the community, I wrestled more with the theological issue
of the place of women in relation to men. I was sure that
the developments in my life were guided by God, yet I seemed
to be moving away from what I had regarded as the Christian
teaching about women. Now I winced at or avoided altogether
the Pauline passages requiring a woman's submission at home
and silence in church. I accepted eldership in the local Presbyterian church, the first woman among its session members,
and even preached on a Sunday.

At home I agonized over my relationship with my husband.
"It is the duty of a wife to obey her husband—even if she
thinks he is mistaken—and leave the consequences to God."
So counseled a Christian leader early in our marriage. Absurd,
I reasoned. Why, even the obedience of children to parents
in the New Testament carries the condition "in the Lord."
What did the "headship" of the husband mean? My own honor-
ing of the principle, following my mother's example, meant
that I placed unwarranted pressure on my husband to act ra-
tionally, function efficiently, and be accountable for the affairs
of the family—even to the point of relinquishing my own responsibility. That increased neither his love nor respect for
me.

Meanwhile, my maturing self recognized his fellow humanity, his needs and his feelings, the areas of his weakness and the limits to his strengths. I saw that while he excelled in some things I had the advantage in others, that we could complement each other and grow in cooperation. Surely I should expect my developing experiences as a Christian to be in harmony with the truth of Scripture, not in divergence from it.

Resolution began with reading Helmut Thielicke's *Ethics of Sex*, particularly where he describes the social background of Christ's day and the revolutionary nature of Jesus' dealings with women. Further study for a sermon I gave on Mother's Day in International Women's Year (1975) lit up for me the thrust of Scripture with regard to women. The injunction in Genesis, "Your husband shall rule over you," is part of the curse which Christ came to undo. The restoring of women to responsible partnership with men is part of God's redeeming process in the world.

I saw also that Christ cancelled for his disciples the traditional concept of dominance and submission. "It shall not be so with you," he said. "Whoever wants to be great must be your servant, and whoever would be first must be the willing slave of all" (Matt. 20:26–27, NEB). My quarrel with the apostle Paul's view of a husband's headship ended at that point.

My understanding of Paul was also greatly increased at the Washington Conference of November 1975, when "biblical feminists" from North America met for the first time. As we looked at his practical instructions for the family and matched them with the social conditions of his readers, we saw how wisely and graciously he dealt with them. I asked myself: If Paul were addressing himself to men and women today, would he not write in a different vein? Would he not adapt his advice to our conditions as he did to theirs?

Paul's words came with healing to his readers then; if today they bring strife and resentment, surely it is that we are misusing them—lifting them out of context and applying them unaltered to ourselves. Because of that conference, I now find the congruence I sought between what I was learning in my own experience and what God was saying in Scripture. The outstanding women of the Bible were not aberrant exceptions to the rule but pacesetters in the way God wants us to go. I can come to the Bible and find myself not put down but raised up.

My mother-in-law does not share my change of vision. "I didn't think there was anything Christian about Women's Liberation" she wrote when she heard about the Washington conference. Well-versed in the Bible and loyal to the conservative view of women, she was expressing, though mildly, her shock and dismay at my participation. I chose my reply for her reassurance, to point out that my position was true to Scripture. "Among the first Christian feminists," I wrote to her, "were Mary, sister of Martha, and Priscilla, wife of Aquila."

My emergence to a more active role outside the home has meant a continuing readjustment in the family. Graham has always helped me: it was part of the tradition of his parents' family that the males did the dishes, and he knew more about babies than I did. He led our three boys in taking their share of household jobs but they helped grudgingly. I wanted them to take more responsibility but found it hard to give up the controls.

Recently I was hospitalized for an operation and went to Jamaica to convalesce. That was a salutary experience for all of us. Our fifteen-year-old turned out to be an efficient manager and a good cook. Now I can leave him a note about the menu and he will cheerfully take charge of the evening meal, after school, while I catch up on shopping or visiting. Our twelve-year-old, obviously more aware of the tedium of repetitive jobs, has obliging moments of largesse: "Mummy, I'll give you five minutes of my time to clear away these dishes" is typical of his concessions to drudgery.

I savor every expression of appreciation. "I didn't realize how much you did until you were away." This, from Graham, who has quietly dropped his demands for a uniformly high standard of meals and house-care.

I too have changed. Forcefully divorced from my routine, I have given thought to reordering my priorities. I now take more time to share my husband's passion for gardening. Perhaps that was really what he wanted of me when he carped at details of dust and disorder and resented my evenings out. With more give-and-take between us, I can begin to see him with more sympathy, as someone like myself, subject to process.

We all went out one evening except Graham. As we prepared to go, he was standing at the sink over the debris of dinner. "Everyone's leaving me!" he cried, his voice full of dismay. Instead of rushing to relieve him, I stood my ground but remarked with unusual mildness: "Yes, I know what that feels like—to be left behind with the chores."

Later, reflecting on centuries of male privilege, I was glad I was gentle with my husband in his resistance to our temporary reversal of roles. It took years for me to come to terms with drudgery, and I still balk at being housebound. Can I expect him to change his attitudes any more quickly?

Chapter Three

Mildred Meythaler

I HAVE NEVER called myself a feminist nor thought of myself as one. The only women's groups I have belonged to are AAUW (American Association of University Women) and the missionary society at church. I have never marched or picketed. Once I watched a program about fasting Victorian suffragettes being force-fed in English prisons; it was frightening. I knew I lacked their courage. Yet in the sixties I was surprised to see myself, and my mother-in-law and grandmother, in the pages of *The Feminine Mystique*.

A number of people in a variety of contexts have asked me if I am a "women's libber." It's the kind of question I feel I ought to say "yes" to. Think of the liberation of Dachau. Are you a Dachau libber? Yet there has been something about the tone of that question, something denigrating about the use of the term "libber." It makes me cautious about answering "yes" while—so far as it depends on me (Rom. 12:18)—I am trying to live peaceably in white, prosperous, suburban, middle-class America.

Browsing one day at the University of Wisconsin library, I

Mildred Meythaler, a graduate of the University of Wisconsin, mildly fore-shadowed the current "biblical feminist" movement with a 1960 article in HIS *magazine (see Appendix). A librarian, she lives with her husband Jerry and two teen-age sons in Waukesha, Wisconsin.*

began reading *The New Feminist Movement* by M. W. Carden. Carden had analyzed the hundreds of women across the country who were active in the "women's movement." The emerging profile was so like me it was startling.

This characteristic woman is almost always a college graduate. She has trouble finding a congenial gynecologist. She is married. She cares about etiquette even when she serves simple meals. She introduces strangers. These descriptions were especially interesting to me because they characterized me as well as belied the speculation that the women's movement was characterized by men-haters, lesbians, and other deviant types.

But for me, Carden's most cogent point was this: potential recruits for the women's movement are those women who feel most acutely the conflict between traditional feminine virtues (dependency, unassertiveness, adaptability) and the values of the larger American society (aggressiveness, competitiveness, individualism) to which they have been educated. That's me.

I was plunged into that conflict on my first job after graduating from the University of Wisconsin. I discovered that a single man on the faculty had been paid more than I, although he had less experience. It was my first experience with an unfair labor practice, and it hurt. My idealism (and naiveté) left me unprepared. I resolved never to sign another contract with the school under such conditions, and I didn't. Today I seem to have lost that simplicity of mind. Juxtapose that action against my present caution.

Someone once jokingly called me the "first biblical feminist." (Move over, Eve.) Still, I was becoming something like that long before I knew the terminology and long before the women's movement surfaced in middle-class America. An article I wrote called "Women's Work" appeared in *HIS* magazine in January 1960. That was early, even avant-garde, for such ideas to appear in an evangelical Christian publication—or in the mind of an evangelical Christian.

It has been interesting to me to reexamine that article after it has been buried for seventeen years in an inaccessible attic file. What would I change after these years of housewifery, motherhood, and church membership?

First, this sentence: "The greatest service . . . is to raise children who love the Lord Jesus"—which I wrote before we had any children. I would now say, "The greatest service that any Christian couple can offer is to love God first and then each other."

A second change touches on the subordination of women to men. The tremendous import of Galatians 3:28 and Ephesians 5:21 had not yet broken through my mind-set. At that time I was coming out of and reacting to the church of my childhood in which women dominated men. I then followed the reactionary swing of fundamentalist churches to the other extreme: the domination of women by men. I now understand that neither extreme is biblical.

Twenty years of marriage have brought me to my senses. Both the church and the world contrived to teach me that marriage was the Promised Land. They encouraged me to idolize my husband. I have come to see what a cruel and impossible burden that laid on him. I have come to see marriage as still part of the "wilderness" experience, as is every relationship and experience, that we might look beyond the disappointments into eternity.

The women's movement has helped me to realize these things. It has encouraged me to appropriate the freedom for which Christ has set us free (Gal. 5:1). Within the past year I said to a small group in church, "Women's liberation has helped women—even church women—in many ways." An educated, married Christian male looked me right in the eye and said with papal authority, "No Christian home can be happy if the wife is a 'women's libber.'" What could I reply? In previous discussions my husband and I had freely shared problems that we faced. This man now had the simple solution to our problems. I might well have answered "But that is tantamount to saying, 'No Christian home can be happy if the wife is a follower of Jesus, because Jesus is a 'women's libber.'" But I didn't. That man's hostility caught me at a tired, discouraged moment, and years of conditioning took over. I started to cry.

The interesting thing about my response was that although I despised myself for coping in that fashion, no one else did. Everyone was sympathetic. Another man in the group rose gallantly to my defense. Tears were a far more acceptable answer (traditionally feminine) than an honest forthright reply (traditionally masculine) that would have brought us closer to the issues.

Recently I attended a church service where a dramatized reading was given, warning women of the dangers of life. A svelte young woman with long blonde hair, wearing black Danskins, danced out life's dangers, one of which was alcoholism; another, women's liberation. The dancer donned men's pants, pulled out a cigar, and puffed out her ridicule. The church roared with laughter. One might expect that Christians, having been ridiculed themselves by people who haven't taken the trouble to find out what Christianity is all about, would be careful not to pass on the same treatment to others. But it is clear that as the women's movement has developed and grown, misunderstanding of it and hostility to it have mounted in the conservative Christian church.

Have you ever played "Bible Football"? Last year we attended a neighborhood church group, and on one frigid winter evening when the attendance was down, our male leader brought out the game. Now to most Christian men, it simply brings together two of their favorite things. The leader promptly divided us into two groups, men against women. Immediately I was in inner turmoil. I wanted to be on the same team as my husband. (Men hate to lose. Women lose by winning.) Defections were not allowed, however, and the game was on. Questions were fired at us, questions that required a very specific knowledge of the Bible to answer correctly. And so the competition raged: touchdowns, field goals, extra points, the works.

It was a terrible experience. A baby Christian was trampled; a nonbeliever was ruthlessly exposed; a slow thinker was cruelly embarrassed (never to return). When we evaluated the game on another evening with our leader, he was surprised. He found competition exciting, and winning, exhilarating. I do not. Women's liberation has frequently been distorted *(e.g.,* the Danskin dancer) as women now wanting to compete with men. Wanting to win and wanting to be free are two quite different things in my mind.

The truth of the matter is that I have repudiated competition altogether. I thank my sons for that. During their childhood they sought me out for a million games: Monopoly, checkers, chess, Clue, Scrabble, Sorry, Flinch, ping pong, Rook, Authors, Battleship, Feely Meely, Careers, Life, Dominoes, tennis, golf, softball, Pick Up Sticks . . . you name it, I've played it. They loved to win, and I loved to have them win. Success makes for success. I thought I was doing them a great service by instilling them with a success mentality as early as possible. Then came the day when some Christian men criticized me harshly for "letting them win." "That's dishonest," they said.

About that time I began to see the folly of the competitive mentality, whether in Youth for Christ Bible contests or Awana basketball games, whether in business or education or professional sports. I have given up competing. I realize this is far easier for a woman to do than for a man. Recently, I offered to call my husband to help a man who was working hard on a difficult project. I said something like "My husband is very good at . . ." The man responded, to my complete surprise, "I give up. He wins." That incident impressed me all over again with the intrinsic part that competition plays in American maleness—and therefore in American society at large. Clarifying my feelings about it has been important to me, as I have felt the hostility toward the women's movement within the church.

Apparently some Christians feel that there is a question about a Christian woman being at all sympathetic to or involved in the contemporary women's movement. My first response to that is that a Christian must try to right wrongs. I am supportive of many "liberationist" goals for the same reason that I am actively trying to do something about civil rights, world hunger, anti-Semitism, and the need for teachers' unions. There are wrongs to be challenged, evils to be combatted. Jesus came to set captives free. The church can no longer support Bible-reading slave owners. I may or may not be the one wronged. It's as simple as that.

I support liberationist ideals for a second reason: personal, historical reality does not honestly allow me to do anything else. The sovereign God of history wove these ideals into my life. God did not make me in the fundamentalist church's image of the ideal Christian woman, *i.e.,* petite, pretty, clothes-conscious, musical, nonintellectual, good with small children, shy in public.

Early in our marriage my husband and I were asked to speak at a church one Sunday night. He was to speak to the college group; I was to speak to the intermediates (fourth-fifth-sixth graders). For me it was a fiasco. As a bachelor the previous summer, my husband had already proved himself a genius with intermediate scamps at daily vacation Bible school. Still, the mores of that church did not allow the planners (or us, for that matter) to raise the question beforehand of who was suited for what, according to the gifts that God had given us. It was assumed that a woman would be better with the younger group.

I suppose, though, that my most disillusioning and feminism-inducing experiences with the church over the last years have revolved around ideas of physical beauty. My birth and early years in the Christian faith were deeply immersed in university intellectualism and the austerity of British-born Inter-Varsity Christian Fellowship. Consequently I was not prepared for the preoccupation with outward beauty that grips the conservative church. By turns I overlooked it, denied it, excused it. Even as a teen-age nominal Christian, I had been influenced by Romans 12:1–2. Its practical denial by the conservative churches into which my conversion led me was something I couldn't consciously acknowledge.

My first church experience after conversion was dominated by a woman, the minister's wife, who was very pretty. Beyond that, her clothes were tight, her necklines low, and she whisked around in a yellow convertible. One of her specialties was dancing on table tops—in a restaurant, in the church basement. To my amazement, the church people loved it. Her husband was proud to have her by his side. That type of experience, repeated with variations, had a profound effect upon me. It launched me into what could be called my beauty period.

I was not going to hurt the Kingdom by being a mousy Christian. I returned my hair to the blonde that God had originally made it. I lost weight. I learned to use contact lenses. I had my nose repaired (it had been damaged in an automobile accident). In retrospect it seems both funny and pathetic to see the kind of concoction one can produce by mixing biblical teaching with the pressures of life. Ostensibly my rationale went something like this: my husband loved me and married me as I was; now I would be beautiful for him. He had married Leah, but he would find that he also had Rachel.

Looking back upon that time, I feel a terrible sense of degradation. My beauty plunge, I suppose, judged within the framework of its own values, was successful. On several occasions I was referred to as "our Doris Day." More than one male made himself available. Friends, bless their misguided hearts, even said "movie star"—just what they'd said about my husband when they viewed our wedding pictures.

I learned, or relearned, several things from that period:

- —The utter deception of beauty. A beautiful woman, like a handsome man, can be a very difficult person to live with.
- —The banality of beauty. Preoccupation with beauty leads to viewing human beings as objects to be used.

Feminist experiences, you see.

If beauty is exalted in conservative church women, then intelligence is certainly deplored. Our second church experience came as members of a large, metropolitan, Baptist church. They were difficult years for me. The women of the church, if they went beyond housewifery, were secretaries, nurses, Welcome Wagon ladies, Avon callers, symphony volunteers. The women teachers (elementary, of course) were without exception single. To my knowledge I never encountered another married woman in that church who was a college graduate, although many of the men were. The women tended the nurseries, directed the children's choirs, played the piano and organ, sang, or worked in the missionary society, quilting, sewing, baking.

That might be called my trying-to-be-an-acceptable-fundamentalist-church-woman period. I now had the beauty parlor habit as well as an enviable collection of recipes. I had two radiantly healthy (thank you, Jesus) boys who helped me understand and like small children. (Cynicism aside, this is a real testimony to the transforming grace of God.) I sewed and knitted clothes for the boys and myself and derived a lot of satisfaction from it. I practiced the piano regularly and enjoyed it. I

read to the boys, exercised at the Y, and got so I could put
together an acceptable dinner party. Still, I was different. Only
one married woman of the church risked "guilt by association"
to offer herself in friendship. I earned a little mad money by
working one day a week, then two, as a librarian in a nearby
school.

I suppose I might have continued on indefinitely that way
if my husband had not taken a job overseas in a mission school.
The months we spent abroad were landmark ones for me: they
changed me unmistakably, dramatically, irrevocably. My ideas
of the mission field (beyond St. Paul's) had largely come from
reading about Hudson Taylor, James Fraser, Amy Carmichael,
Borden of Yale, all pioneers. Because we were short-termers,
we didn't have the orientation or the language given to "lifers."
And I had just come from a "woman's-place-is-in-the-home"
church. Those three things meant I was bound to have a shock
or two.

I remember the anger I once felt at Hollywood and James
Michener when I saw Julie Andrews standing in the sands of
Hawaii making Boston baked beans for her New England missionary husband. I thought it was a caricature. Abroad myself,
on a mission field, I was appalled to see how close it was to
the truth. Missionary men, virtually without exception, expected their wives to maintain twentieth-century American
standards of fashion, cleanliness, and hospitality, without twentieth-century incomes or accommodations. I resumed my
beauty parlor habits. I had to have formal evening dresses custom made, since none could be purchased and it had not occurred to me to take any with me.

I recall one missionary husband sharply criticizing his wife
in front of us because her hair was frizzy. That, when the humidity as well as the temperature were constantly in the 90's.
I recall women in girdles and evening dresses accompanied
by men in short sleeves and no ties. When I discussed it with
the leader of our mission who had traveled the world over,
he told me that he found it standard practice. Men, comfortable; women, uncomfortable.

Another difficulty revolved around my "place." There was
a "desperate need" for a librarian at the school. I was put
under tremendous pressure to work full-time at the school,

in spite of the many difficulties I was encountering trying to
run our household in a foreign culture with no knowledge of
the language. If the school had provided me with a full-time
maid, I would have been willing to try teaching—although
there would still have been many difficulties. Maids are often
more of a problem than a solution for women accustomed to
doing their own work in privacy, and maids who barely speak
a word of one's language can be a job in themselves. However,
the school did not offer to do that, and our finances did not
allow it, so a maid was not the answer.

I either had to try to do both jobs at once or weather the
storm of criticism that staying at home would bring. A decisive
factor in my decision to stay home was the kindergarten
teacher of the previous year. She wanted to teach, but the
school would not allow her to because of the horrendous problems her family had; a home-life in wreckage is a poor witness,
they told her. One would have thought that on the basis of
that experience, I would have been urged to stay at home.
But such was not the case.

However, the political situation in the country was so tense,
our economic situation so precarious, and my husband's work
load so heavy, that I could not escape the conviction that my
main job was to provide a home for the family that would
be a refuge from storms. That is what I tried to do, although
I was a great disappointment to some. The same people who
wanted me home at home wanted me at school abroad.

In the end, our time abroad was a very good experience
for me. When the dust had settled, I was able to acknowledge
for the first time that there were as many problems with the
fundamentalist Christian church as there were with the liberal
Christian church out of which I had come. Both had their foun-
dations largely in the shifting sands of expediency. I could look
at that fantastic collection of fashionable hats I had bought in
biblical obedience in the fifties, now collecting dust in the attic,
and laugh. I was freed to face the differences between church
authority and God's authority over my life. I started to read
the Bible with new eyes. I was freed to start thinking all over
again what it meant to be God's woman alone. So you see
what a liberating experience it was for me.

But apart from our church involvement in the U.S. and on

the mission field overseas, at least two other experiences have had a deep influence on me. The first is the home in which I grew up: all female, except for my father. My childhood years were happy ones. Since I was the youngest, I marked the end of my father's hopes for a son. Still, I never felt he loved me the less. Since there were no brothers, the responsibilities and privileges of our household during my formative years had no sexual differentiations. My mother sent the laundry out and worked part-time with my father at his place of business when things got busy. In turn, my father cooked his German specialties and often ran a dust mop around because my mother didn't get to it. They shared the yard and garden work. Although my father had initially hoped for sons, he provided my sisters and me with every opportunity for self-fulfillment that he would have given sons—and in the end, he seemed satisfied. He did all this in spite of the patriarchal German clan in which we moved, who told him on more than one occasion that he could have bought a farm (the zenith in their minds) with the money he had tied up in the education of his daughters.

The security and confidence that this type of nonsexist rearing gave me had far-reaching implications. It led me to go to college for an education as well as (perhaps) for a husband. It enabled me to graduate, husbandless, and support myself for a time without too great a sense of panic. And even in marriage it gave me a backdrop of security to know that I could, if it were ever necessary, return to a job at which I could support our children.

Not that my father ever relished the idea of spinster daughters. He was an inveterate mental matchmaker and frequently pointed out likely prospects. My mother, on the other hand, rejoiced that her daughters had a choice that neither she nor my grandmother had had: to marry or not to marry. Beyond that, however, our ability to support ourselves was a special source of satisfaction to her. Her father had died when she was six, and she and her mother had faced a terrible struggle to survive in their rural American context. Only because my grandmother had married was her brother required by law to share the family inheritance with her. If she had remained single, she would have been totally dependent on his good will and generosity. So my mother knew from her own experience how important adequate job training could be for a woman.

Finally, I now live in an essentially male household, dog included. Since we have only sons, we have had a chance to reexperience my nonsexist rearing—except that the shoe is on the other foot. This has provided us all with much food for thought. How are we going to share the work around the house, especially those tasks traditionally thought of as "woman's work"? Should mother still be working at eight o'clock in the evening while dad reads the paper and the kids watch television? Theoretically, no. But changing the pattern is another thing.

Since my husband has always worked "for the night is coming when man works no more," I never felt strongly that he should be helping a lot around the house. He worked hard, and I worked hard. The problem came in trying to get the boys to do routine household chores. They resisted, and with my husband gone much of the time, I had to be a marine sergeant to get things accomplished. Neither my husband nor I like this role for me.

As we have wrestled with these problems over the years, I suppose we were really forced to come to grips with them when I was offered a full-time job as school librarian. Returning from overseas, my husband had started a business of his own, which launched us into a financial security that precluded my having to work for money. With all the conveniences of American society, an experienced, motivated housekeeper can keep the home fires burning quite brightly and find additional satisfaction working at a part-time job, without being frustrated or constantly exhausted. A full-time job is another matter. A new arrangement has to be made within the household. Shall we look for a maid? Shall I quit the job so we can forget the hassle? Is it good for anyone to be exempted from sharing in the countless chores that are low-status and have to be done over and over and over? Is it good for one person to do them all? These and many other questions come up for consideration.

I wish I could say that our family has worked through these questions to a final solution. I can't. A few things have helped. We bought a dishwasher and a large freezer. We hire someone to do the weekly cleaning. I cook; my husband and sons clean up. We pray. We entertain during the summer, not during the school year. We have given up the idea of a constantly neat house. We buy only wash-and-wear clothes. We eat out oftener. We try to share one another's burdens.

Sometimes we succeed. Sometimes we fail. But that is what life was like before—which brings us beyond feminism to the human condition. It's easy to blame sexuality, blame institutions, blame history, blame genes, blame anyone and anything but ourselves for what we are and where we find ourselves. Sometimes we get away with our accusations; sometimes they are justified. Nevertheless, blaming is not productive.

Being a biblical feminist, or a potential recruit for the women's movement, or whatever, has helped me to face myself more realistically. It has forced me to think once more about what kind of a human being I am and what kind I want to be. It has made me look again at what kind of relationship God wants me to have with my family. How can I better appropriate the light and power of God within me? How does God want me to invest the remaining days, months, years, of my life? Why do I enjoy so many good things in life? Why do I daily experience little surges of happiness? These are some questions I face today. This is where I am now.

Chapter Four

Judith Ann Craig Piper

BEGINNING SEMINARY in 1975, the International Women's Year, was symbolic for me—not because I'd been suddenly liberated and decided to do graduate work, but because I was at last moving into the field of endeavor that I had spent my life moving toward.

We had just left the Midwest, where I was considered a far-left liberal, and moved to Berkeley, where those same beliefs and ideas were almost off the scale to the right. A new job for my husband, new schools for the children—and the movers had lost three of my most important kitchen boxes. . . . On Orientation Day at the Graduate Theological Union I felt anything but oriented. I went into the empty chapel and sat down to collect my thoughts.

As I looked down at my Bible my eye fell on Romans 9:16,17. In the Moffatt translation I had with me that day it read:

You see, it is not a question of human will or effort but of the divine mercy. Why, scripture says to Pharaoh, "It was for this that

---

Judith Ann Craig Piper, R.N., a veteran of the U.S. Army, is a third-year ministerial student at San Francisco Theological Seminary. She and her husband Daniel hope to serve God overseas. The Pipers have three children, Mark Edward, Mary-Esther, and Rosann.

I raised you up, to display my power in you, and to spread news
of my name over all the earth."

I began thinking back to some of the major ways in which
God's loving providence had led me to that moment.

The attitudes toward women that surrounded my birth and
early childhood were developed from the necessities of pioneer
life in the territory of Wyoming. Relatives on both sides of
my family had filed claims for homesteads in Wyoming, the
first place in the world to grant women's suffrage. As people
moved west in the early days, the hardships of pioneer life
demanded that everyone work together to make a living re-
gardless of age or sex. With homes, barns, and fences to be
built, plowing and planting to be done, and cattle to be protected, women took their places beside men to do what they
were able to do to further the common life. One aunt took
her turn riding the range to guard the cattle, packing a pistol
she was well qualified to use.

As people worked together, the citizens of the territory realized that women were working their full share to develop the
land. That "open" attitude was reflected in Wyoming's first
constitution (1869) and its nickname, "the Equality State." So
the women in my ancestry were used to being treated as full
citizens. My great-great-grandmother had her own weaving
business; my great-grandmother worked in the coal mines to
help her husband through seminary. My mother remembers
going for her first automobile ride as a preschooler in 1914,
when her mother, grandmother, and aunt, along with her father and uncle, were given a ride to town to vote in a state
election.

Women were also involved in the development of schools,
churches, and local government. The first community building
to go up was always the schoolhouse. After it was ready for
use, it was typical for a small group of citizens to invite someone
to start a Sunday school there and hold worship services. It
wasn't unusual for a woman to be asked to pioneer that community church effort.

My great-grandparents heard that there was a Christian
rancher at a not-too-distant homestead whose wife, Elizabeth
Wolff, was a minister. They invited her to begin Sunday school

at the schoolhouse and to start a prayer meeting in their home.
From her ministry I can begin to trace the first direct spiritual
input into my life. She was responsible for bringing many of
my relatives to Christ and forming their attitudes toward faith
and life.

By the early thirties when my mother and father had married
and moved into the small town of Newcastle, they invited Sister
Wolff to come start a church there. After meeting in a home
for a few years, several families wanted to erect a church building. They were able to buy the small hotel of a nearby mining
ghost-town and took it down board by board to load on a truck
and take it into town. Besides the pastor, other women like
my mother, my aunt, and grandmother helped dismantle the
old building, pound out the nails, and straighten them to save
for the reconstruction. When I asked mother recently what
she wore to do this work she answered "Pants—same as the
rest!" which expressed the matter-of-fact way in which she
looked at the kind of life style she had grown up with in
Wyoming.

As the people worked together to erect the building, they
were expecting God to expand the congregation so they built
a larger education wing than they needed at the time. This
they made into an apartment which was rented to my parents.
That's where I was born in 1940—in a church, a church pastored by a woman, a church of resourceful, energetic people
who were willing to follow the leading of the Holy Spirit in
developing a community of Christians who loved each other
and would reach out to people around them with the gospel
of Christ.

When World War II began, my dad went on active duty
and was stationed in Washington state. There we attended a
church also pastored by a woman, Sister Garrett. Many women
had been involved in pioneer church planting in the west and
were still active pastors until after World War II. Those
churches of my early childhood were from the Wesleyan/Holi-
ness tradition. The people in that denomination (Church of
God—Anderson, Indiana) accepted all the gifts of the Holy
Spirit as valid for today, and healing was well known among
them, but they had rejected an active use of the gift of tongues
because of abuses of that gift. They believed that all the gifts

of the Spirit were given to women as well as to men and consequently women could also be called to be ordained. They also believed that since the purpose of the gifts is to equip Christians for ministry, all Christians are called to minister.

Because of that kind of theology of the church and its mission, my parents were somewhat prepared for a heavy assignment God was going to give them. In 1946 my dad received orders for Dutch Harbor in the Aleutian Islands. Since the population of neither the Navy nor the Army on the island was sufficient to warrant a military chaplain, my father, a master sergeant at the time, was asked by the commander to do what he could to provide for the spiritual needs of the people on our island, supported by the Methodist missionary on the next island. That arrangement hadn't lasted long before the mission board called the missionary to mainland Alaska and my family was asked to do what they could on that island as well.

Work to be done for God—and people willing to do it in the power and wisdom he would provide: that philosophy of ministry saw my parents through a year of serving both the military and civilians on the Aleutian chain. That the "people" were laymen and laywomen and even children made no difference. The fact that the fields were "white unto harvest and the laborers were few" meant that all who loved Jesus must roll up their sleeves and get to work. That philosophy launched me on my career of service to others for the Lord's sake. Though I was only six, I was given my share of work to do: singing in the children's choir, explaining things to children with questions, inviting them to Sunday school—and, best of all, pulling the rope of the mission bell which called Aleut children from all over the island to the mission Sunday school.

When the missionaries had to leave, my mother was asked to take over a radio broadcast. Mother accepted the job with "fear and trembling." She asked the Lord to help her bring glory to his name through that unfamiliar work. A gruff sailor instructed her, "Don't rattle your paper into the mike," and that was the extent of her formal preparation for her radio ministry. But her preparation in the Spirit was constant. She would ask the Lord for the message he wanted to give through her that week. We children prayed for her and for the listeners. Every week Daddy typed her script and taped it to cardboard "so it wouldn't rattle." Each Wednesday evening after a quick supper we glued our ears to the radio. "Good evening, friends," she always began—and I was thrilled to be her "friend." Mother preached the gospel on the radio on Wednesday. Daddy preached the gospel in the chapel on Sunday.

By the time we moved to Guam in the Mariana Islands, where my parents became associated with the work of Baptist missionaries, I was getting a pretty good idea that Christians of all denominations were concerned to share the gospel. The Guamanian culture was strongly Spanish-Catholic as a result of early mission work there. Our Aleutian chain had borne the imprint of the early Russian Orthodox missions, and my own background was shaped by the revivalism on the U.S. frontier. I also had a pretty good idea that the ministry of women in missions was not only welcome but actually indispensable to the work of proclaiming the good news of Jesus Christ and carrying out the social implications of the gospel.

When we returned to the States we moved to Morro Bay, California, at that time a small fishing village with a choice of four churches: Catholic, Episcopal, Assembly of God, and Presbyterian. My parents chose the Presbyterian as representing the church closest to our beliefs. That interested me. What did I really believe? Even though I was only in junior high, because of my background I was ready to tie down my basic theology. The Lord had just the person to help me do it: my Sunday school teacher, a missionary recently returned from China. A woman of great energy and conviction, she successfully combined a ministry in the church with a ministry to her family. Because two of her children were friends of mine from Christian Endeavor, I was often in their home, where I observed her living out the gospel she was sharing on Sunday morning. As hostess for her physician husband, mother to her six children, daughter to her aged mother who lived with them, and person concerned for her community, she seemed to have a quiet, balanced ministry that touched many people in a lasting way with the love of Jesus.

In my high school years we were overseas again, this time in Europe. There my parents were associated with a Huguenot mission which deepened my roots in the Reformed tradition and, along with the ministries of Keswick and Capernwray, deepened my unconscious conviction that the work of God is done by willing human hands empowered by the Spirit of God. But my simple view of men, women, children, laity, and clergy alike being called to ministry wasn't to last much longer. Naively, I thought that since our family had lived with and loved and worked with Christians of many denominations in many parts of the world, our experience was normal.

For my senior year, my brother and I returned to the States as boarding students at a Christian high school. There I began to realize that not everyone held our view of "inclusive ministry" when I entered into a discussion in the dorm about the Fall Spiritual Emphasis Week speaker. The school had invited an evangelist, and I had been taking notes every day in chapel because I wanted to capture some of the joy and power with which she opened the Scriptures to us. I had always enjoyed theological discussions, so I joined in that one expecting to hear views that would contrast and round out what we had heard from the pulpit. It was one of the deep shocks of my spiritual life to find that they were discussing not her interpretation of Scripture or delivery but whether she as a woman should be an evangelist. My eyes were opened. It was the beginning of an awareness that was to become acutely painful in later years: the Body of Christ was deeply torn because of a fundamental difference of opinion. Some Christians felt very strongly, sincerely, and scripturally that the work of women in God's Kingdom was limited—and some felt very strongly, sincerely, and scripturally that it was not.

The next years passed rapidly as I prepared for a career in missionary nursing. In Lutheran Hospital School of Nursing I met women in all levels in the administration and faculty, women in student government, women directing the spiritual ministries on campus. I met our graduates, who were evangelists, preachers, linguists, and church planters as well as medical missionaries on many fields around the world. I encountered Inter-Varsity Christian Fellowship, which in many ways held a view of ministry similar to the one I was familiar with from my background. Women were included in full-time staff positions and greatly aided the students as we attempted to evangelize and minister to our campus community.

A fairly open attitude toward women in ministry has been

characteristic of Inter-Varsity since its early days. They were among the first Americans to welcome the ministry of Corrie Ten Boom; other women Bible teachers, writers, and editors have strongly influenced the lives of many student generations for Christ. Experiencing I-V staff people encouraging and facilitating the ministries of women staff and students, I felt the acceptance and love of both the Christian community and the Lord as I was being trained to serve God on my campus and in my work after graduation.

Following graduation I was a candidate with a mission board whose policy required registered nurses to have a couple of years of nursing experience before leaving for a foreign assignment. As I prayed about it, I felt that active duty with the Army Nurse Corps would give me a wide range of professional experience as well as involve me in a ministry with young people. My father swore me in for a two-year "hitch" during the Viet Nam War.

Growing up as the only daughter with two brothers in the family, surrounded predominantly by men, I had experienced a sense of specialness about femininity, a sense of being cherished, a sense of being gifted with a quality of existence that was needed to minister wholeness and humanness to those around me. I remember sensing that first as a preschooler during World War II. My father had invited a few Italian prisoners of war to our home for dinner. As one of the young officers (who had taught me how to eat spaghetti) bounced me on his knee, he said, "I have a little girl about your size back in Italy." I was aware that my presence as a *girl* had brought him both joy and pain and I "prayed in my heart" that Jesus wouldn't let it be too long until he could see her again. With comments like "You remind me of my kid sister" or "That's one of my sweetheart's favorite Bible verses" or "Just like my mom's cooking," I knew that my mother and I shared a ministry to servicemen that gave them a firmer platform for their spiritual growth than they otherwise might have had.

In the military community I felt accepted and respected as an individual person. There was an exciting sense of camaraderie even in basic training. There were four other colonels' daughters in addition to myself in our class, and we remarked on the unexpected sense of fulfillment we now experienced as being a real part of it all. People in the military expect change, and my family had had an active part in the military's changing attitudes toward women—from accepting them alongside, to accepting them as integral parts. (Someday there would be women at the academies; deep in my heart I had dreamed of being the first woman chaplain in the Army.)

One happy surprise of Army life was the number of Christian women in our Basic Training class of one hundred nurses. There were about twenty Christians and about half of them felt that God had called them into the Army as a specific ministry. It was encouraging to all of us to realize that we weren't alone in our call to serve God in the Army Nurse Corps. Besides looking for Christian classmates in chapel, we tried to notice who said grace in mess hall and who was drinking straight Coke at "happy hour." The encounter I remember best was walking down the hall of the bachelor officers' quarters and seeing an I-V *Hymns* on someone's desk. I couldn't wait for her to return so I grabbed the book and ran up and down the hall asking everybody who it belonged to! It didn't take many antics like that until you could find the other Christians just by asking who were the "religious fanatics in this outfit"!

Our group of nurses began meeting for Bible study with the Officers' Christian Fellowship where we met other people who had formerly been associated with Inter-Varsity Christian Fellowship, and who also considered the military as their mission field. There, we as Christian women experienced a healing sense of fulfillment. We were included on a team that was dedicated to evangelizing and discipling the Armed Services. We experienced a living out of the OCF motto, "all one in Christ Jesus" (Gal. 3:28). It's difficult to put into words, but it hits me now in a similar way when I'm able to use my gift for teaching as part of a team ministry—rather than standing by waiting for an invitation to make cookies.

As a single woman in the military I had felt that my ministry was well accepted. But at the post where I was reassigned after my marriage, I was surprised by the pressure I felt to conform to the more traditionally "feminine" forms of ministry to serve military personnel. That, with the escalation of the war (which meant longer shifts and fewer days off), and the beginning stages of an illness that was nearly to cost my life before it was diagnosed, combined to put an end to any active ministry as I had known it. It was the beginning of a "dark night" in which I was to discover that God's love for me didn't depend on whether I could work for him or not—and it didn't depend on the acceptance or rejection of other Christians.

My husband Daniel and I were discharged from the Army about the same time and were eager to get on with our plans toward the mission field. Dan had been a campus staff person for Inter-Varsity and through I-V had gained a real concern for missions. At Michigan State he worked on a Ph.D. in natural resource economics, hoping to teach at a foreign university after graduation. Those years are a bad blur to me. My health continued to deteriorate under the avalanche of child-rearing. Our two oldest children often needed nursing care around the clock. It was at that period of my life that I was most hurt by the philosophy of Christian womanhood characterized today by the *Total Woman* mentality. I was in a struggle for survival for myself and my children and my husband's career. I was waging a battle as a wife and mother and being made to feel like a *total failure* because I couldn't keep up a middle-class personal appearance and house—and because my mind was so rattled I couldn't come off with the niceties of conversation.

The physicians were finally able to diagnose my illness, and Daniel finished his doctorate about the same time. Overseas work was out for the time being, so Dan took a job in the Midwest. After about a year of medical treatment I was feeling like attempting to be a human being again—which for me meant some form of ministry. It was like waking up from a bad dream to find myself in another one. Women at our church there didn't even vote, let alone teach Bible classes. When I was asked to lead a small interdenominational group that met in a home, some of the women were forbidden by their husbands to come because it wasn't "lawful" for a woman to "teach" Scripture.

On faith (and in a state of culture shock) I applied to Grace College of the Bible in Omaha to complete a degree in missionary nursing. A week after my graduation Daniel was invited to work on water problems in California, and the Lord thus opened the door for me to go to seminary.

Many happy surprises were in store for me at San Francisco Theological Seminary. One was that nearly half my class was comprised of women. Another was the openness I found on the part of a good many people in my church to my being in the M.Div. (ordination) program at seminary. That openness was the result of a lot of consciousness-raising by several women and men before I came.

In Berkeley I've had good and bad experiences as a woman seminarian, but mostly good. I'm sometimes asked, "What does your husband think of what you're doing?" I try to answer something like, "Well, he believes the family should come before career. That's the way he does his work and he expects the same from me." It is a common experience for me as a seminarian to be with a male classmate and have people talk to him about theology and ministry and simply ignore my presence and/or my professional interests. Having accustomed myself to this, I assumed that one woman was referring to my colleague when she told a group that "We have a near-minister in our midst" and I was totally unprepared for her grimace and the surly tone of her final comment, "and it's a she!"

In my first two years at seminary I have diligently worked through the passages of Scripture that apply to family life and to ministry. God has called me to serve him and that is my goal—not ordination. However, if I'm called by God and a group of Christians to serve them in an ordained capacity, I want to be sure that there are no scriptural impediments to my answering that call.

A principle of Christian living that has always been important to me is "not eating meat" if that will cause a problem for another Christian. Love among Christians has been more important to me than my personal views. I can be a "teetotaler" for the sake of love. I tried, when at my predominantly pacifist Mennonite Bible college, not to make a big deal about being a veteran. I've worked hard at building bridges of Christian love between the Calvinists and Arminians in my life.

But "not causing problems" for other Christians in the case of the "woman's issue" means giving up what God has asked me to be and to do. I've suffered a lot and cried a lot about the pain I've brought to some others in the Body of Christ by staying in seminary and continuing as a candidate for ordination. It hurts, too, when some of these people feel that I'm "rebelling against God's order" or destroying my "high view of Scripture" or encouraging a "gnostic view" of the Incarnation or embracing "demonic biblical feminism" or following "blind pride." Some of these same men and women have contributed in the past to my physical and psychological health. Others have taught me the Scriptures which I hope to share in my ministry, and it's a hard decision to have to wound them. One of the most painful aspects is the pressure I feel from people who think it is quite legitimate for me to be a foreign missionary (my husband Dan still has opportunities for overseas work) but refuse to recognize the same ministry in this country as valid if my health prevents our going abroad.

I believe that God made me a woman for the same reason that he made Jesus a man: in my generation and in my geography this gender enables me best to carry out the work he has called me to do. I probably don't fit the stereotype for a woman in my culture any better than Jesus did for a man in his culture. I see that as simply an occupational hazard for both of us—but it didn't prevent him from getting his work done.

Chapter Five

Lorraine Peters

GOD IN CHRIST has broken the barriers between male and female. That discovery revolutionized my life after years of searching and struggling. It was like breathing fresh spring air after a long, hard, prairie winter. In many ways my journey into life has just begun.

My earliest memories go back to the vast Canadian prairies of Saskatchewan, inviting me to run, skip, and play. My brothers and I spent carefree hours climbing haystacks, playing hide-and-seek, and periodically tending our neighbor's cattle. I was awed by the fiery sunsets and sometimes wondered about the Force that controlled such a breathtaking display of color. God was a mystery to me. I remember snuggling up to my mother in bed one cold wintry morning and asking her "Where is God? Is he a man?"

My father, a rural schoolteacher, taught in one-room schools and was responsible for thirty or forty pupils ranging from grades one to eight. It took ingenuity to make the lessons interesting and understandable. Children came to school on horse-

---

Lorraine Neufeld Peters, R.N., studied Bible at Multnomah School of the Bible, and linguistics at the University of Washington. After serving as missionaries in Brazil with the Unevangelized Fields Mission, she and her husband John now live in Waterloo, Ontario. Together they lead marriage enrichment and family seminars.

back or in horse-drawn carts, traveling three or four miles.
As a family we attended the local Mennonite Brethren church
every Sunday morning, where my father, usually the choir
director, could draw music out of the most unpromising singers.
God came alive for me when I heard songs sung in worship.
In our home we had daily Bible reading, prayer, and singing—
activities as unquestioned a part of our family life as our parents'
love for us.

It was common for evangelists to travel around the prairies,
holding meetings in various communities. One night I was attending such a meeting with my family. Even though, as a
child of nine, I understood little of what was being said, I suddenly became deeply troubled. In desperation I ran out to
our car. My uncle, who was also at the meeting, sensed my
distress and followed me. My younger brother was already
in the car, so my uncle talked to both of us. He said something about God caring for us and loving us, and that God
would come into our hearts if we invited him in. I was unsure of what that meant, but in my childish way I cried out
to God for help. A sense of calm and well-being came over
me. I was filled with love. I even felt warm toward my younger
brother.

When I was twelve years old, my father was invited to become principal of a Christian high school. Our family moved
to what used to be an Air Force training base in the southern
prairies. Students from Canada and the United States came
to take three years of Bible training or to attend the high school.
Most of the students lived in dormitories in that isolated community, and our family lived in an apartment on the same
campus.

I worked hard at being a good girl. Since my father was
principal, I felt I had little choice but to behave. I secretly
envied and admired my friends who dared to break the restrictive rules. I had no such freedom. Sometimes it made me angry,
but I couldn't admit it.

Students of that institution were expected to attend all scheduled meetings, whether for prayer, Bible study, or hearing missionary speakers. Christian commitment was judged primarily
by the degree to which one participated in those and other
events considered important. A theme I heard repeated many

times was the call to missionary service. To serve God, particularly in jungle areas of a foreign country, was the highest Christian calling. I had little doubt that some day I would live and work in such a place as a missionary nurse.

After high school I spent three years in nurses' training in British Columbia. There I was active in the Nurses Christian Fellowship and became president of our local group in my last year of training. I was impressed by the vitality of the Christian women who were our sponsors and staff workers. Their love of life and of God made an indelible impression upon me.

My vision to become a missionary was rekindled during my last year of nurses' training, when I was attracted to a young man in his first year at the university. We came from similar backgrounds, but John was different from others I had met. Although he claimed a personal faith in God, he was not so prone to accept traditional Christian ideology or life styles— which both intrigued and frustrated me. Why couldn't he be content with the simple faith I professed? John had applied to a mission board for pioneer missionary work in the jungles of Brazil, and before long we decided to make it a joint venture. We were young, idealistic, in love, and ready to conquer the Amazon jungle for Christ.

Before that dream could be realized, each of us had further training to pursue. I took a concentrated Bible study course, followed by a summer of intensive linguistic training. John left for Brazil a year ahead of me. In the meantime I visited churches and friends, to tell about my anticipated missionary involvement; many of them became our financial and prayer supporters during our years in Brazil.

John and I were married seven months after I arrived there. Automatically we assumed the traditional family roles: John, as head of the household, made the major decisions; I, his wife, deferred to him. It was the Christian way as we understood it. Fortunately, John was sensitive to my needs and wishes and seldom went ahead without at least seeking my opinion. In some ways the arrangement was comfortable; it relieved me of making difficult judgments. But that attitude sometimes frustrated John, who wanted me to think for myself and in some cases make my own decisions.

Shortly after our marriage we flew into the jungle to establish our first home. The Shirishana, among whom we had come to live, were patient with us as we struggled to learn their language. They had a sense of humor that carried us through many embarrassing situations. Conflicts between our culture and theirs were obvious. We had many possessions, they had few. We liked privacy, they all lived together in a communal house. They shared their goods, we did not. What did I have to offer, I wondered.

The spirit world was real to the Shirishana. They believed that evil spirits caused death and had to be dealt with. On more than one occasion we were called to treat someone who was ill, after the witch doctor had tried unsuccessfully to heal that person. We gave medicines, sometimes to no avail. Then would come the test. If God is Spirit and Life, couldn't he intervene if we committed the situation to him? With fear and trembling we cried out to God in stumbling Shirishana words, admitting our helplessness. More than once, people were healed, much to our awe. But there were other instances when witchcraft, praying, and giving medicines all came to naught. Even little children died.

Slowly, imperceptibly, we sensed the Shirishana beginning to trust us. They were intrigued by John's and my behavior toward one another. In preparing a meal, for instance, if I burned the meat, they were amazed that John did not beat me in anger. Loving and respecting one's wife was unheard of in that culture. The wife's duty was to bear children, bring home produce from the fields, and cook. If a baby girl was born, she was labeled a female dog and was sometimes killed. As I came to understand their situation, I began to love those women. Occasionally I felt them trusting me in return. Perhaps that is what God was about, in me and in them. The love of Christ could overcome cultural barriers.

After eight years in Brazil, by then with a family of four children, both John and I sensed an inner restlessness about our ministry. Even though two years were scheduled before our furlough was due, we felt compelled to leave our mission post earlier. But who would understand such a move? Hadn't I been taught all my life that being a pioneer missionary was God's highest calling? Hadn't I obeyed that call, giving my entire life to that vocation? Finally, in desperation I poured out my jumbled thoughts to God. If no one else understood, perhaps he would. It was my only hope. A sense of calm came over me. I could leave Brazil in peace, without worrying about the reactions of other missionaries and the Christian constituency in North America.

There is truth in the statement that the life of a missionary is characterized by faith. Yet in some respects our faith in God has been tested to a greater degree since leaving the security of that mission organization. Coming home to the Canadian prairies in the middle of winter and with no assurance of a home could be viewed as a foolish way to test one's faith. We were overwhelmed, however, to have a house offered us in the same city where my parents were living. Friends rallied around and donated the furniture and clothes we needed.

It soon became clear that further study, at least for John, was necessary for whatever lay ahead. Five months later we moved to Illinois, where he completed his B.A. and M.A. degrees. Then we moved to Michigan, where he enrolled in a doctoral program in sociology. Living in a racially mixed neighborhood exposed us to an explosive world about which we had only heard and read. John quickly became involved in his studies, and our children adjusted to the racially mixed school with little difficulty.

Even with a baby at home, I immediately became involved in the public school system as a volunteer, to find out what was going on in the community. At my first meeting, I struck up a conversation with a woman who intrigued me immediately. It was obvious that Jane was a sensitive and caring person, and it turned out that we were to see much of each other during the next three years.

The more John realized what lay ahead of him, the more concerned he became that I be aware of how his Christian world and life view were being changed and shaped. One way to facilitate that was by my getting to know his colleagues and professors. Our missionary experience intrigued them. I anticipated condemnation but instead found respect and admiration when they found out that I had survived in the jungle with young children.

During our second year in Michigan, a young black minister

named Malcolm gave a course in black history at a Presbyterian church. That course opened my eyes to social injustice as nothing had before. My comfortable Christian faith was shaken. Malcolm told of how he had agonized to accept himself as he was, in a predominantly white society.

Another event that shattered my complacency was the introduction of a busing system to achieve racial desegregation in the public schools. Deep-seated hostilities suddenly exploded. The barriers seemed insurmountable. But out of the turmoil came honest attempts to establish lines of communication. In an effort to ease the tensions, my friend Jane, for instance, organized a group of parents, black and white, to talk to the principal of the school our children were attending. I admired her courage and gave her my support.

In an attempt to build trust among the school children, a social worker in our local school initiated a program in which, on Friday afternoons during school time, children chose a "fun" activity to pursue under the supervision of an adult volunteer. I had a cooking class in my home and was excited to see children from different backgrounds accept each other and have fun together. As chairperson of a volunteer mothers' group in the school, I asked the principal about expanding the program. He agreed, and many mothers, some fathers, and university students became involved. Enthusiasm generated from the program soon spilled over into the children's schoolwork as well. Even my own children were excited about my participation.

As my self-awareness increased through my involvement in the community, a subtle change took place in the way John and I related to each other. We began accepting each other as two unique individuals, each with certain capabilities. Unknowingly, we were beginning to relate to each other as equals. We were freer to love one another, have fun together, and express divergent views. We were adding a new dimension to our marriage.

One of the issues John and I began discussing was the "women's liberation movement." I had paid little attention to it, because I thought it had nothing to say to me. I was happily married and enjoyed being the mother of five children. My husband even encouraged my outside activities, as long as they didn't interfere with the running of the home. From time to time, my friend Jane and I would also discuss the women's liberation movement, in which she was active. At first I couldn't understand her involvement. She too seemed happily married, with an open relationship with her husband and children.

Two issues I found I could support were "equal pay for equal work," and trying to overcome the bias in elementary school texts, which showed boys involved in exciting activities but girls only doing housework. Reading *The Feminine Mystique* by Betty Friedan, I empathized with suburban housewives who had no stimulating outlet outside their homes. I was shocked to learn of the advertising media's deliberate attempts to keep women preoccupied with housekeeping and in making themselves attractive to men. No wonder women weren't developing their mental capabilities to the fullest, if they accepted such a philosophy.

By that time John had completed his studies and had accepted a teaching position at a university in Ontario. As I contemplated our return to Canada, I knew I would never be the same again. Too much had happened. The complacent Christianity I had known was inadequate—yet, deep down inside I believed that God loved and cared.

In Ontario, life was different. Everything seemed so easy. People appeared content with the pursuit of money, beautiful homes, and affluence. With my husband earning a faculty salary, I found myself being enticed into accepting such values. But, although I enjoyed getting to know my neighbors, I felt a vacuum inside. I began to understand the "unhappy housewife syndrome." I realized it would be wrong for me to restrict my activities to my home and family, much as I loved them. I knew I had to become involved in the community, working with people, whoever they were. I knew I had something to offer.

I became involved as a volunteer with the Children's Aid Society. A social worker and I met with mothers who were having difficulty coping with their children. Many of the women were single parents who felt defeated and who had no sense of direction. They often vented their frustration on their children. Through films, discussion, and just listening, we tried to suggest ways in which they could more effectively deal with their situations. Occasionally we saw these women helping each other. I was learning more than I was able to give.

Then I accepted an invitation to speak to a women's group on the changing role of women. At that time I was also introduced to a course called "The Philosophy of Christian Womanhood." A glance through the course materials left me devastated. It assumed that women were married, that their duty and fulfillment lay in motherhood, housekeeping, building up the male "ego," and "submitting" to their husbands. Scripture verses were used to reinforce that philosophy. A thousand questions raced through my mind. My search regarding the place of women from a biblical perspective began in earnest that day.

Several months earlier we had received material that spoke about "evangelical feminism." I discovered that other Christian women and men were struggling with the same questions that had been raised in my mind. Not only that, these writers were affirming equality between male and female as a fact of the Christian faith. I was amazed to learn that some of the women in the eighteenth and nineteenth centuries who stood up for women's rights did so because of their commitment to Christ. I wondered why I hadn't been exposed to such facts from my own Christian heritage.

I still feared, however, to search the Bible seriously about the "woman question." I knotted up inside when I thought about passages that had traditionally been interpreted to emphasize the total submission of women to men. Finally I had the courage to study Christ's behavior with women. It seemed a good place to start. I was excited to see that Jesus talked openly with women about deep truths, that he traveled with them and allowed them to touch him in public—all of which were culturally unacceptable in that day.

The more I read, the more eager I became to present my findings to that church women's group. When I presented my talk, I was baffled by the apparent apathy and even resistance to my perspective. I was in turmoil for several days after that. Was I wrong? I didn't know where to turn. My husband was understanding, but the battle was mine.

I mulled over the words in Galatians 3:28—"there is neither male nor female, for you are all one in Christ Jesus" (RSV). I thought about the revolutionary act of Christ's appearing first to women after his resurrection, telling them to inform the men about the most important event in history. The implications were staggering.

Then, in the midst of my agony came release, so complete and profound that at first I knew nothing but awe. Hymns that told of freedom and liberty came spontaneously to mind. Suddenly I understood that life in Christ meant freedom for men and women alike. I was the most liberated and excited woman on earth.

In the days and weeks that followed, I became increasingly aware of changes taking place in my attitude and actions. I experienced strength and peace and an intense desire to be "all I was meant to be." I was able to share with John the excitement of my self-discovery. I began to see strength in my children that I hadn't noticed before. I found myself wanting to affirm the strengths of others and to reach out to people who were hurting. I became intolerant of injustice and developed a thirst for knowledge. When I read the Bible, it was as if my blinded eyes had been opened to discover new truths about God and his dealing with mankind. I even gained courage to study those difficult passages that dealt with relationships between men and women. (A book that helped me in this area was *All We're Meant to Be* by Letha Scanzoni and Nancy Hardesty.)

Testing has been an inevitable part of discovering my identity in Christ. The conflicts are real and often intense, but I have found a solid base from which to deal with the complexities of life. Coming to know God means that I have an obligation and desire to develop and use my abilities. It is wrong to hide behind my husband's or children's identities—or to manipulate them to gain my own ends. Accepting myself means making my own decisions and taking responsibility for my actions. In practice, this can be painful.

When John's and my desires conflict, we work out a mutual agreement. We love and trust each other enough that neither one of us feels the need always to be the winner. As John has become more aware of what is involved in running a household, he has assumed more of the responsibilities I once had (such as preparing breakfast). Talking about our feelings, encouraging and challenging one another, is more important now than ever before. Yet we have been amazed at the pain we have had to go through in order to accept each other as whole partners in every sense, after having lived and accepted the traditional marriage roles with their subtle expectations. I have had John's support and he has had mine as together we have agonized before God about which way to go. But the pain is ultimately worth it.

In relating to our children, I find it exciting to tell them about my discoveries and involvements. They share my enthusiasm by telling me about their activities. Sometimes they even share their innermost thoughts. Both our sons and daughters are expected to help with household duties. Insisting on this has sometimes made me feel guilty, especially when neighborhood children aren't given similar responsibilities in their homes. But our children are coming to understand that it is a "just" arrangement.

Outwardly, the changes in our family structure may appear insignificant, since most of my activity still revolves around my family. At times I have been insensitive to their needs in trying to live out my new-found freedom, yet gradually I am learning to use it responsibly. I am convinced that a woman finds her true identity when she discovers, as I did, that God has broken the barrier between male and female. In Christ she is released from having to fit a prescribed mold.

Chapter Six

Frances Adeney

SILVERY BITS OF fluff rose in the sunlight out of my tiny hand. They sparkled through the sky as the wind caught them, taking them higher. I stood watching, my blue wicker doll carriage filled with enough milkweed pods to last the morning. The sun warmed me as I worked, releasing the captured bits of silver hidden in each dark cradle. The early morning birdsongs were company enough.

A sharp call broke into my reverie. My mother's disapproval, the wet sheets hanging on the line, and the "misuse" of my new birthday doll carriage all bombarded my consciousness. Yes, there were bits of milkweed fluff sticking to the neatly hung washing. Yes, the carriage was muddy and bedraggled after its trip to the back field. There was no doubt that Mother was upset. For me, a four-year-old, the morning had ended.

Many years passed before I understood my mom's frustration. Each Christmas brought a new doll, each birthday a new dress. Between times I ran around with my older and younger broth-

Frances Adeney and her husband Bernard are world travelers now rooted in Berkeley, California. Together they are involved in counseling, directing worship, and occasional teaching in the House Church of Berkeley. Fran also teaches in the Crucible, an educational ministry of the Berkeley Christian Coalition.

ers, building hideouts, playing cowboys or cops and robbers, having rock fights with the neighborhood bullies. Mother was always ready to console me when I was labeled "just a girl" and excluded from some of the more adventurous neighborhood escapades.

My parents had a way of accepting me that was crucial to my development and self-confidence. They didn't push their expectations so hard that I had to fight them in order to become myself. As the dolls stacked up in the closet, I climbed trees and played baseball. But I never wished I was a boy. My parents loved me as a person, not just as their "little girl."

Nevertheless, it was usually the boys who helped Dad with building projects. They carried lumber and pounded nails, learning skills and gathering information. I was more fragile and protected, always given the benefit of the doubt, never spanked. As a child I accepted that role-stereotyping very readily. I planted a rock garden, went berry-picking, learned to sew, began cooking and baking. I also spent hours reading or riding my bike to some lonely spot in the Illinois countryside.

My early public school education was not unique. Failure by the schools to encourage critical thinking caused children to accept the status quo rather than question it. I did well academically and socially so I had little reason to ask hard questions. As I moved into high school, the results of that tendency became more detrimental. Role-stereotyping for girls pushed me away from interest in the sciences or manual arts. Math, too, was something that didn't seem to matter much. Cheerleading, dating, and girlfriends were a big part of my life. I drifted.

My parents sensed an underlying boredom in my attitudes, and it was they who rescued me from the high school quagmire. They searched for a college that would accept me one year early and succeeded in finding one. Not particularly eager to conclude my butterfly existence, I nonetheless accepted the challenge of college at seventeen. An added pressure in that direction was my younger brother's acceptance by the same college that year.

Mother and Dad expected me to succeed academically and pursue a career, but again I was unwittingly discouraged from the sciences and other male-dominated fields. Preparation for those professions often took many years; what I basically needed, as my folks saw it, was something practical I could "fall back on" in case I didn't get married, or if "anything happened" to my husband. Had my parents' outlook been broader, or had my education been of a better quality, or had I myself been a less self-satisfied person, I might have insisted on considering more alternatives. As it was, I looked only into nursing, teaching, and social work—a limited career horizon.

I was still very family-oriented during my college years. I had little appreciation for what I saw going on in the university dating world. Somehow I had gotten through the butterfly stage and knew that honest relationships and real encounters were more valuable than the dating games all around me. Usually I spent the week going to classes, working, and spending time with my brothers or a few friends. Most weekends I went home.

During that time, the self-confidence my parents had instilled in me helped me a great deal. I never became a wallflower in my own mind. Although lonely at times, I knew I didn't need a "date" to be a worthwhile person. For this I feel a true sense of gratitude to my parents. They never pushed me to bring home boyfriends or to find the right man (although marriage was certainly part of their vision for me). They encouraged me to study as long as I wished. They never doubted my ability to do what I had set out to do.

I have said little about Christianity in all this. But much of the credit for my sense of freedom and personal worth as a young person should go directly to God. I learned to love him at an early age and thus learned my worth as an eternal unique person created and loved by the Master of the universe. The church, however, seemed to have a more narrow outlook. There was little encouragement to become creative and outgoing, and much emphasis upon being modest, meek, and silent in church meetings. On the other hand, my status before God was never lowered; I was never taught to be ashamed of my sex or to consider myself a second-class citizen in his Kingdom.

I continued in the same church structure until adulthood, learning much, questioning little. A certain dichotomy between my spiritual and secular life enabled me to be assertive and outgoing in other circumstances, while remaining quiet and accepting within the church. I accepted the church conventions but by my actions denied their implications for my total life.

A major turning point came when I met Bernard Adeney, whom I later married. I was out of college teaching grade school at the time. Our first long talk concerned the question, "Who am I?" My insular uncritical background had left me totally empty of the inclination to ask such a question. I was fascinated. Through our relationship I began to learn to question, to probe, to notice and evaluate many areas of my life. And then my struggle with sexism began. A person is not troubled by what he or she is unaware of. My experience with the doll carriage, the trivial dating in high school, the limited learning opportunities I had seen as possible for myself—none of those experiences had been interpreted in my mind in any way at all. Even now, I wouldn't knock them solely into a sexist category, for life is complex and multidimensional. Simple labels are elusive at best, harmful at worst. But I began to see that cultural conditioning of all sorts, including sex-conditioning, had been steering me throughout my life in certain "acceptable" directions.

Furthermore, being considered "just a girl" didn't necessarily end with childhood, as I soon discovered in the professional world. In my first teaching job, pay and respect were equal for both sexes. The principal of my school, the only man on the immediate scene, regarded me more professionally than I, a beginning teacher, regarded myself. In fact, he recommended me for a very responsible job of leadership in a summer educational program: I was to direct and critique a team of five teachers as they learned the art of team-teaching. I arrived on the scene full of anticipation and excitement, anxious to share my training and knowledge of team-teaching which I had been gathering during the two years following my master's degree. I was greeted with an immediate demotion. The man in charge explained to me that since I was so young, older teachers would find it difficult to accept my leadership and direction. I would therefore not be teaching the group of teachers, but rather would become a learner in the situation.

The group I was to lead consisted of four women and one man. The man had neither educational background nor experience in team-teaching. He was not one of the older members of the group, yet he was given my position as leader and instructor for the summer course. I was told that my pay would remain the same because it was in the written contract, but I must engage in the group as a participant and allow this untrained man to direct it.

I argued that my sex, age, and experience were all known when I was hired for the position. My leadership role was as much a part of the written contract as my salary. But such reasoning brought only a cold look and a repeat of the change in plans for the summer. I felt humiliated and trapped. I had already rented an apartment and moved to that Milwaukee suburb. I needed the income. The change seemed devoid of reason to my mind, but I was helpless before it. I lived through the summer, making the best of a bad situation, trying to quell my resentment and to benefit in some way from the program. That was my initiation into the world of professional discrimination against women.

Never before had I considered my sex or my youth to be handicaps, and I refused now to begin seeing them as such. I continued in the teaching field for another three years. Perhaps because I was working with young children and most of my colleagues were women, I didn't again experience such a painful situation. The few men I worked with did respect me professionally. I was given free rein in the classroom to use methods and content that varied from the given texts. My advice about certain disturbed children was taken seriously. I was treated as an equal and a contemporary. Perhaps teaching is a field in which women have already made enough of a mark to have gained such respect.

In the context of the church, my childhood acceptance of norms for Christian women broke into rebellion in adulthood against distorted concepts of meekness and male "headship." I began to see that a woman's complete silence in the church was a selective interpretation not consistent with either Jesus' view of women or with the real-life practice of the apostle Paul. It became clear that meekness meant something deeper and more challenging than being silent or maintaining a doormat mentality. Headship, too, took on greater dimensions in light of Jesus' ways with people and Paul's exhortations for husbands to love self-givingly as Christ loved. Mutual submission as a basic tenet in marriage meant that a man's headship in the family could be beautifully centered on service and care rather than dominance. These insights exhilarated me. I believe that deeper, richer meanings, quite different from the stereotypes I learned as a child, are in God's Word. Along with other Christian women and men who have become sensitized to these matters, I continue to ferret out the meanings—knowing that God's wisdom is not outdated or culturally contained.

Marriage brought the traditional views on women to a very personal relevance in my life. How Bernie and I saw our marital relationship theologically and culturally would play a large part in determining the nature of our life together. We began our marriage nine years ago with the traditionally conservative outlook about women in the church and home—though, from the start, we diverged from the generally accepted cultural outworkings of those ideas.

During our first three years of marriage, Bernie went to the University of Wisconsin and I taught school. Although I was the "breadwinner" and he the "head," we made plans and decisions together. After our time in Wisconsin we traveled in Europe, studying and interacting with wandering Americans. A highlight of our nomadic year was a four-month stay at L'Abri Fellowship in Switzerland. Together we studied, managed a small chalet, led a daily Bible study, and discussed Christianity, sometimes far into the night. We walked side by side, not one in front of the other.

Mutual respect and love under God were at the base of our relationship. We acted in accord with those basics even when cultural conditioning of the church or society pulled us in other directions. Tyrannical or childish ways of relating to one another were not part of our ideal of Christian marriage. We desired our life style to reflect attitudes of cooperation and service rather than competition and constant struggle. Bernie didn't dominate the relationship or tell me what to do. I didn't expect him to make every decision.

As we lived together we more frequently questioned the status quo, and our individual roles in marriage were no exception. We did not follow the man-at-work, woman-at-home system of life together. We thought that attempting to move in the same direction in our pursuits would enable us to maintain a closer, more understanding relationship. Study and travel helped us develop our thinking along these lines and gave us mutual experiences which drew us closer. (I often wonder how couples manage, who live totally separate daily lives. We try hard to live one life together as two distinct persons.)

Following our travel in Europe, we spent two years studying theology at a small community center in Singapore called the Discipleship Training Center. There, although women deferred to men in details of etiquette, women taught in churches, traveled as speakers, went out as missionaries, and studied theology. Among those educated Asians, there was more equality than in the conservative churches I'd seen in Europe, England, and America. (Among the general Asian church populace, however, the churches were still male-dominated.)

Those years were rich learning experiences for both of us. They also brought the birth of our first child and the adoption of our second. We often say that I went through the first pregnancy and Bernie went through the second—since his prayers and labor to adopt another little girl were so intense and exciting. The children have added immeasurably to our family; they have added pressures as well as joys. One of us had to give up study. My decision not to complete my second year of theological study in Singapore was a difficult one, yet I enjoyed caring for our babies, only seven months apart, during that year.

The following year saw us trekking to London so that Bernie could complete his B.D. program at London University. It was a hard period, as the home/work role divisions we had so far avoided seemed inevitable. Bernie needed to study intensely to finish his course, which I really wanted him to do. Still, that left me frustrated as a full-time mother in a London suburb. I had little contact with people of common interests and little time to pursue anything but scrambling babies.

That year in London showed me clearly that identifying myself solely as a wife and mother was not enough. I was excited about my children but bored with friendships with other mothers that continued on a trivial level. I was fascinated with my children's creativity and development but harried by washing nappies and walking two miles to the grocer's with two infants. At times, when Bernie returned home from college at six, it seemed like a week since he had left at eight that morning.

A central area of struggle in our early years of marriage resurfaced during that time: conflict over the seemingly minor area of household chores. When we were first married I worked full-time and was actively involved in Inter-Varsity Christian Fellowship. Bernie was a student, and a strong leader in the I-V chapter. Although his schedule was much more flexible, I still found myself responsible for the care of our apartment, cooking, laundry, etc. Cultural conditioning had pretty much determined our marital roles, and we hadn't yet begun to question them.

Bernie was willing to share in the household tasks but had a very marginal concept of what was necessary in the upkeep of a home. Having lived at boarding school and then in a college dorm, there was a lot he didn't see at all. He honestly felt he was doing half the work by doing dishes and occasionally tidying the house. His expectations from a wife no doubt unconsciously included being cooked for, cared for, and laundered once a week. I wasn't much better off. After a 7:30–4:30 day at school plus two hours on campus, I still cooked hot meals every evening. My own background dictated it as part of a woman's duty, and as yet I wasn't free enough to dispense with that part of the "wife" routine.

Two things were happening. First, our expectations of one another were locked into stereotyped roles. Bernie thought he should "help me" with the house—i.e., it was really *my* job despite the role reversal in the economic area. Yet he did want to be fair. I expected Bernie to be aware of all that needed to be done and always to act maturely in carrying a good share of the load. Needless to say, we had a few fireworks over these expectations.

Second, our individual self-images complicated the problem. To the extent that my identity was wrapped up in my role as a "good wife," it was hard for me to give up some areas of household work. I was plagued with guilt because I couldn't maintain high housekeeping standards. I couldn't let go of "wifely" responsibilities and accept Bernie's criteria of a job well done. Looking back at that period, it still isn't easy for me to be objective; it seems to me now, however, that my own cultural conditioning led me to place a higher value on certain homemaking activities than was realistic in my situation. Basing my self-worth too heavily upon performance of those tasks kept pushing me to excel in them as well as in professional and social areas. The strain showed.

The situation we faced in London brought out those old conflicts, but by then we were more skillful in handling the tensions they engendered. Since our relationship had become more stable, I was able to give over a few areas of responsibility to Bernie. He in turn had a fuller grasp of what was involved in caring for a home and two children. A lot less of our individual self-worth remained vested in the male-female stereotypes imposed by society. But despite the more mature handling of our London situation, both of us wanted the strict division of roles to be only a temporary arrangement. We could see that for us it did not foster closeness or mutual encouragement.

As we looked to the future, therefore, we determined to work in a way that would allow flexibility and a certain amount of role-sharing. Our London experience helped us look purposefully for a life style that would reunite our daily routines. We asked God to lead us to a kind of work in which we both could be participants. He brought us to Berkeley, California, to the Berkeley Christian Coalition.

In Berkeley our Christian community supports us in our marriage and in our attempts to develop a life style that allows for individual development and mutual participation in family life. Besides emotional support, they offer us practical help. We never lack a loving babysitter when we need one. Friends help us with gardening. Help with housecleaning is always available. The Christians here are consciously trying to love each other in practical ways, sharing life with one another, offering their God-given gifts freely to one another. Living in this kind of extended Christian family has helped us much, offering possibilities for utilizing our talents that would have been impossible in a "nuclear family" situation.

The Coalition, too, has allowed us to share responsibilities and to work together. We have each been encouraged to take on more work, or less, as our family needs change. A result has been a far greater sharing of work around the home on an ongoing basis. One of Bernie's strongest gifts is his compassionate fathering ability. He has learned to cook and takes an active part in the less glamorous tasks about the house. We each take responsibility for certain jobs we do most efficiently. Our sharing is no longer "helping out the wife" but a truer life together.

I don't mean to imply that our struggles are ended. Being ready to exchange responsibilities or take on new ones as the need arises is an integral part of this kind of sharing. A few months ago a third child was born into our family; the demands of a new baby tie me down greatly these days. I see this as a time for Bernie to take on most of our community commitments. He will bear the major burdens of teaching and directing the Crucible (a local Christian "free university"), working with our housechurch, participating in the organization and growth of the Coalition. I will shoulder more of the home responsibilities and child care. For now, this is a happy situation for us both. In six months to a year, however, the situation will change again. I will want to reinvolve myself with the larger community, and Bernie will need to share more of the work load at home.

That kind of flexibility is difficult but rewarding. For example, it hasn't been easy to find time to write this chapter. Seemingly minor skirmishes with the clock hide deeper issues of priorities and psychological pressures. Time is merely the surface issue: how to find hours of quiet in a hectic family, church, and work schedule. Other dilemmas lie beneath the surface. What comes first in my own life? In the lives of my husband and children? Traditionally, the husband has been given freedom to pursue intellectual activities, so it takes a sensitive, unselfish, and psychologically strong man to encourage his wife to excel intellectually.

To wrestle with these priorities, though, has been worthwhile for us. Looking at ourselves, our roles, and our mutual expectations has been extremely painful at times. But through it we have expanded our view of ourselves, each other, and our potential as a couple. I am beginning to have a sense of the significance of life, a wonder at what God has done in creating unique persons who can make choices. And I am determined to choose, not to drift—to form with Bernie our own history with God's guidance, and not to be limited by history's mistakes.

Chapter Seven

Sharon Gallagher

BEING RAISED FEMALE in the post-World War II period didn't cause any problems for me in itself. Because of an illness my father developed in his late twenties, my mother was forced into a more active role in our home and in his ministry. She assumed responsibilities usually designated as "male." She did all the driving; she painted rooms and laid linoleum. Her attitude was that she could do anything. Even though women weren't allowed active roles in the church, Mother's ministry wasn't solely one of "helpmeet." She had Good News clubs, women's classes, and speaking engagements. Several times she went to work for Christian organizations.

Perhaps because he had no sons, my father expected me to do anything I wanted with my life. He even joked about my following in his footsteps when I did things he had done in high school, like drama and journalism.

The church I grew up in enforced strict rules of silence in the church for women. Because of that background it was years before I could even pray comfortably in a mixed group. Yet

Sharon Gallagher is editor of an "alternative" Christian newspaper called Radix. *She is a staff member of the Berkeley Christian Coalition in Berkeley, California, and a columnist for* Sojourners *magazine. She is active in the Evangelical Women's Caucus and Evangelicals for Social Action.*

somehow the stronger idea I carried away with me was another concept stressed by that group, the "priesthood of all believers." I got the impression that there was no room for passive bystanders in the Christian faith, and that included me. Also, I was young enough then that I wouldn't have been allowed full participation even if I were male—which probably took the edge off that kind of discrimination.

We lived in the San Fernando Valley in California, about twenty minutes from Hollywood. When I was seventeen, I was bored with school. I won a beauty contest and started modeling. My parents soon intervened, however, and I got out of modeling—which was a good thing. I could see myself becoming more and more of an "object," falling under the neon charm of Hollywood over the hill—which provided just about all the trendsetting in the cultural wasteland of L.A.

In the Christian college I went to, the standards were more middle-class American than Christian. That wasn't something imposed by the faculty but brought with the students from their homes. Looking back on that experience, I can see that much of who I was supposed to be was male-defined. It was an unspoken fact of life that men were valued for what they did: sports, grades, role in student government, professional aspirations—even by the cars they drove. A woman's status was acquired through the men she dated, which depended a lot on how she looked. The social pressure plus the standards held out for us by the media about how to be "O.K." gave us the message that the shade of lipstick we chose was of more value than anything we were or thought.

On the institutional level women were discriminated against in the kinds of hours they had to keep. Senior women had to be in the dorms by ten-thirty on week nights, but even freshman boys had no hours. That was explained by saying that if the women were in, the men would be in, too, which was simply not the case. It was the old "double standard" institutionalized, probably prompted by the fact that girls who "got in trouble" were more visible than boys who did. It was also very easy for males to live off campus but almost impossible for women to get permission to do so. Since it was very expensive to live on campus, such a policy amounted to economic injustice.

Although women were ostensibly in school to get an education, most of them realized that the real message they were getting from home and the college was that they were there to find husbands. This resulted in what was called "senior panic." The women didn't panic because they had to go out to face the world and get a job, but rather because they might graduate without the husband they were supposed to get. That type of thinking was reinforced institutionally by the male/female faculty ratio. Out of a faculty of about thirty-five people, the only female members were the dean of women and the women's P.E. instructor. We were being told, in effect, "Go ahead and get an education, but there are no jobs out there for you."

If the senior panic hadn't been quite so blatant, I might have been caught up in it. But when I saw some women get married, in their panic, to what obviously seemed like the wrong men, the seriousness of the situation hit me. I reacted very negatively against that social pressure. I was also becoming more interested in my studies and was excited by the endless possibilities of life after college.

Possibly because of a certain amount of segregation between the sexes, and because of the heavy role-expectations, male-female relationships at my school were often strained and sometimes silly. I found myself making more friends at a nearby secular university, where role-expectations were more relaxed and where the people I met seemed aware of what was happening in the world—that there was a war in Viet Nam, for instance.

After graduation I moved to the Bay Area to work on a Christian newspaper in Berkeley. At one point a man on the staff asked me to write something on "women's lib." Probably the idea was to evangelize the women in the movement (not a bad idea, in the sense that everybody needs to be evangelized). At any rate, as I read women's literature, beginning with *The Feminine Mystique* by Betty Friedan, I found a name for the anger, rebellion, and loss of sense of self I had felt in college.

As I reread the Bible, whole passages of Scripture became clear to me in new ways. I discovered passages that I had never heard theologized upon by male theologians. I had often heard the verse from Ephesians, "Wives, submit yourselves to your husbands," but not in the context of the whole passage—which begins by saying that Christians are all to submit to one another in the Lord (Eph. 5:21).

An article in a women's anthology discussed how the image on the cover of *Vogue* magazine—a woman with makeup, furs, and jewels—was telling us that we were basically unacceptable as we were The article pointed out that even if that "perfect" image were achieved, women would end up being alienated from the image we were projecting. That helped clarify 1 Peter 3:3 for me: "Let not yours be the outward adorning with braiding of hair, decoration of gold, and wearing of fine clothing . . . " (RSV). The verse wasn't a legalistic ban on certain types of apparel but was emphasizing that those are not the things that are important or essential about a woman.

I also began to find allies. Some were women who had become Christians out of New Left backgrounds, where they had been "liberated" in some sense and saw no reason to give up their personhood on becoming Christians. I discovered other women who had married when they were past thirty after developing a sense of individual identity which they retained after marriage. Up until that time, most of the married women I knew seemed to be nonpersons, living in their husband's shadow, assuming his identity—or at least serving his identity. The marriages I saw that had some degree of equality seemed healthier to me than most others I had seen.

Other allies I discovered were the suffragettes of the last century. In their writings I saw women who based their ideas of liberty and equality firmly on the Bible and on who they were before God: they, too, were made "in his image." Their writings gave me confidence that I wasn't simply doing a twentieth-century gloss on the Bible's stance on women. Later I discovered a long line of "feminist" Christians throughout history, from St. Ambrose to George Fox to Sojourner Truth. The first contemporary woman I read on the subject was Georgia Harkness in *Women in Church and Society*. Although I disagreed with her at points, she raised important questions for me. It was good to see that there were alternative ways to read certain controversial passages. And it was encouraging to find a woman doing exegetical work. Since then, evangelical women closer to my own perspective have wrestled carefully with problem texts, in books such as *All We're Meant to Be* (by Letha Scanzoni and Nancy Hardesty).

Negative experiences also made me more acutely aware of the problem of female identity. I have been the editor of a Christian newspaper for three years. Many of the other staff members are also women. Yet I consistently receive mail addressed "To the Editor. Dear Sir." The person may even claim to have read the paper for some time. The assumption seems to be that a woman wouldn't be in a position of authority in a Christian ministry. We also get letters addressed to the staff as "Dear Brothers," the assumption being that women wouldn't even be involved in a creative ministry. One manuscript came addressed to me as "Mr. Sherren Gallagher." This is not to say that the writer was necessarily a chauvinist-extraordinaire; we have all been conditioned by a sexist society.

There is a riddle that goes something like this: "A little boy was in an accident. His father rushed him to the hospital, where the doctor on duty recognized the boy and called him 'my son.' Who was the doctor?" The answer is, of course, his mother. But I didn't come up with that answer immediately when I first heard the riddle. One day I was reading an article somebody had written about my paper, *Radix*. It said something about "the editor, Sharon," and it gave me a start. Not at seeing my name—but my first reaction was: "Women aren't editors."

I vacillate about the importance of the whole language debate. I've heard uninitiated men slapped down for such slips as saying "girl" rather than "woman" for an adult female. I don't think that grown women should be called girls, yet I've seen women react in ways that could hardly be called "consciousness-raising." Rather, they probably traumatized the man against the women's movement for life, leaving him bewildered and uptight. Language is important, however. Men I have confronted about their use of exclusivist male language—like using the word "men" in referring to members of the church—have often said that such a term is generic and therefore includes women. I'm not sure that women feel included in that designation. Before I became sole editor of *Radix*, I coedited the paper with a man for two years. Other men constantly assumed that being coeditors meant that he was the editor and I was his assistant. I remember being in an editorial meeting with my coeditor when some of the elders of our group (men) were entertaining someone they considered important. They called my male coeditor out of the room and introduced him within my hearing range as the paper's editor while I sat in our office.

I was fortunate throughout all this to have a strong male friend (my coeditor) who helped bolster my self-image and fight for my rights in what was then an all-male structure. If he hadn't been there, I'm not sure what would have happened. When by your very nature you are excluded from decision-making processes, you have no voice, no way of changing anything. At that point, someone who did have a voice had to speak for me. I hope in some way that my experience has sensitized me to helping other people who because of their sex, race, or class may need a voice to speak for them.

As I began to discover how liberating the gospel message was for women, I found other women who were raising similar questions about the validity of traditional male interpretations of the Christian view of women. In response to our shared questions I've led several consciousness-raising groups on "biblical feminism" through an alternative Christian-studies program. Two of these groups were for women only; two others were co-ed (and ended up being mostly male). The two groups that were co-ed reinforced my conviction that, at least initially, women need to be by themselves to discuss these issues. The groups where males were present were male-dominated. Women, it has been pointed out, have been taught not to speak, and often if they are in a group with even a few dominant males, they will remain silent. I also found the co-ed groups to be more argumentative and more objective, in the sense that there was very little personal sharing. There was also more defensiveness in the male-dominated groups; some of the men seemed to feel that to admit female oppression was somehow an admission of personal guilt.

My commitment to biblical feminism has also led me at times to join actions of secular women's groups as a "co-belligerent." At Flamingo Park in Miami Beach some of us participated in such a women's group, one of many political-action groups that had gathered for the 1972 Republican convention (at which Richard Nixon was nominated). The women sponsored

a march in which we, a group of Christian women, didn't participate because of issues like "abortion on demand" and lesbian-
ism. We joined their anti-rape squad, however. Groups of
women would patrol the park all night and approach any
woman who looked as if she was being hassled, to ask her if
she was all right. Some of the women were fairly aggressive
in the way they approached men, causing some men to com-
plain that they felt intimidated. Yet by the end of that week
I experienced more freedom to walk or be out alone at night
in a public place than I had ever felt before.

I'm often unsure about when to be confrontative, especially
with people I don't know well. But in general when I've been
confrontative there have been good results. For example, several years ago another woman and I were asked to represent
our organization at a meeting of representatives of various
Christian organizations working on campus at the University
of California in Berkeley. We were, predictably, the only
women there. When the man who was chairing the meeting
began, he asked if one of us women would take notes. We
refused. I explained that my handwriting was almost illegible
and further that I resented his assumption that all women were
born with secretarial skills. I immediately felt guilty and
thought that maybe I should have assumed the servant role
as a Christian, even though he was wrong. After the meeting
he had a talk with me and thanked me for challenging him.
He said he was just beginning to realize that some of the basic
attitudes about women that he had been raised with were sexist—and wrong.

At times when I've been invited to speak on women's issues
to some evangelical church, it has seemed obvious that the
people were there for a "feminist roast." Sometimes I've felt
like abandoning at least the "establishment" evangelical circles.
And yet there are positive signs. Our housechurch has gone
through many stages and changes in discussing the "women's
issue." When we recently appointed a woman as one of two
elders for the church, a question from someone new to the
group was raised about a woman playing such a significant
role: "Won't her family responsibilities interfere?" It was not
a question asked of the male elder. The man chairing the meeting answered that although we were willing to discuss that

issue privately with anyone concerned, in our church we were committed to the free expression of women's gifts among our body.

Besides a sense of oppression from outside pressures, I carry a considerable excess personal baggage of sexism, some that I'm aware of, probably a lot that I'm not. Now, however, I know that I'm not alone. With other members of my community, I struggle to discern the mind of Christ in regard to sexism in addition to other aspects of our life together.

Chapter Eight

Ruth A. Schmidt

IF I WERE ASKED to play the old game of self-description, I would call myself a Christian, a feminist, and a professor. The relative importance of each term in my self-concept is revealed by the order of those words.

My relationship with Christ as Savior is the most basic fact of my life. As I have on occasion told my agnostic friends, who don't understand the certainty I have about God's existence and love for me, I could sooner doubt *their* existence than that of a Person with whom I have been speaking daily for forty years. If all identifications were stripped from me (and who doesn't consider this possibility in a time of economic difficulties?), my experiential knowledge of God's love and forgiveness would continue to sustain me as a whole person.

Several years ago I wouldn't have given the word *feminist* a prominent place in my self-definition; perhaps I wouldn't even have used it. A feminist is one who believes that women

Ruth A. Schmidt, Ph.D., after over five years as dean of humanities at the State University of New York, Albany, is in her first year as provost and professor of Spanish at Wheaton College, Norton, Massachusetts. She is the author of articles and books on Spanish literature of the nineteenth century and has also written for Christian periodicals. Her landmark article, "Second-Class Citizenship in the Kingdom of God" (see Appendix 2), published by Christianity Today *in 1971, gave new hope to many Christian women around the country.*

are full human beings of equal worth with male human beings and who works to see that realized. Men can also be feminists, so my self-identification as a *woman*, an identification I am proud to make, might be another word added to the above self-description.

True to my culture, which defines people according to the work they do, I describe myself as a professor. I have taught for more than twelve years in colleges and universities; and for five and a half years was an academic dean. Much of my adult life was devoted to preparation for this dual academic career.

The "women's movement," as it came into focus for me during the late sixties, made me come to grips with what I believe is the fundamental social change of our time: full equality for all women. It made me see the implications of this belief in my professional life at the university and also in my participation in the church. I became aware of discrimination in both places. So much work of enlightenment needed to be done. Through my conversations and work with other women of my age and background, it became apparent that I had been extraordinarily fortunate in my life as a woman. I had largely ignored the signals that society sent my way about "women's place" and women's limitations—and hadn't felt discrimination against myself to any hurtful degree. I had pursued my life as I believed God wanted me to, without regard for society's indications that I must conform to a certain role in life.

The reasons for my own development as a feminist stem from my experiences as a preacher's kid growing up in what I would have believed to be a very traditional evangelical Christian household. As a WASP (White Anglo-Saxon Protestant) I would have been counted as part of the mainstream of American life—except that my father started churches for the Christian and Missionary Alliance in small towns in the Midwest where, by the newness of the enterprise and the size of the congregations, I was one of very few young people of my age who had similar beliefs and life style. My parents, of Mennonite background, undoubtedly passed on the heritage of a minority culture to me in many subtle ways (even though they had grown up where Mennonites were the overwhelming majority). I am convinced that it was because of that experience of being an "outsider," a minority person, if you will, that I developed a resistance to what society teaches young women about their role in life.

In my home I was taught that it didn't matter whether everybody else in school did a certain thing. If it was wrong according to the Word of God or my parents' interpretation of it, no unanimity on the part of my peers or their parents would have any effect on the suitability of that activity for me. When as a third grader I wanted to be in the school operetta, there was some debate as to the possible sinfulness of that activity before I was allowed to participate. The decision was affirmative, but my plea that "all the other kids will be in it" had no effect on my father. He said that it didn't matter if everyone else did it; the important question was whether it was right or wrong to do.

So, by being one of the oddballs of my class and surroundings, I learned not to conform to society's dictates. Sometimes it wasn't much fun being "different" at school and on band trips. My social life was very limited. But now I see my early experience of being an outsider as basically important in my formation as a person. It is the view of Romans 12:2—"Don't let the world around you squeeze you into its own mold, but let God remold your minds from within" (Phillips).

Unconsciously, I applied that principle of independence in other areas of life, chiefly in what I thought about my life as a woman in a sexist society and in a sexist church. Since I had also been taught that most churches were quite worldly, lax about, or incorrect in doctrine, and not likely to be completely true to Christ or to God's Word, I had a skeptical attitude toward the life style of most churches. Their customs seemed more cultural than scriptural, and therefore separable from doctrinal essentials. That distinction between the centrality of one's relationship with Christ and the outward expression of Christian faith was heightened when I chose to attend a Christian college that was not in my own narrow tradition. It was a Lutheran institution, Augsburg College, in Minneapolis, Minnesota.

To the credit of my parents, although they had reservations about the Lutheran church and its institutions, they did nothing to discourage my attending a Lutheran college. In their view, Lutherans might be truly "saved," but the Lutheran church in general was pretty dead spiritually; they especially thought this true of the local congregation in our town, where the pastor had done everything possible to discourage the new Alliance church which my father founded and pastored. But as a first-year student at Augsburg, I found exactly the spiritual atmosphere I needed. I was still a minority person as a non-Lutheran, but I was in the majority as a Christian. I finally found many Christian friends of my own age.

I had gone to college without any sense of the importance of a liberal education for its own sake, and, coming from a poor preacher's family, I knew I needed to learn how to do something that would enable me to earn a living when I graduated. My concern about preparing for some job shows that I didn't think of college as a place to find a husband who would be the answer to all life's problems. On the other hand, my idea of women's jobs was very narrow. I *did* want to be good at whatever I chose to do, for—although I didn't have the patience to do things as meticulously as my father always insisted I do them—I did have the desire to excel at something. If I started to cut corners, to use nails instead of drilling holes and using screws on some toy or project, my dad would remind me, "If it's worth doing at all, it's worth doing well." (I'm aware now, of course, that having no brothers, and only an older sister who was also enterprising, I had a chance to do a wider range of things than if the tasks had been divided between brothers and sisters in my home.)

All I knew for sure about my vocational choice when I started college was that I didn't want to be a teacher. Yet God guided me in the direction of teaching anyway, through the example of an English professor. What a role model Anne Pederson was for me. Sitting in her Survey of English Literature class, I thought, "If one (I?) could teach like Miss Pederson, it wouldn't be so bad to be a teacher." Although I wasn't convinced that I wanted to be a teacher until I plunged into it after graduation, I now know how important that first vision of a whole person was for my choices and incentive to succeed. Here was someone whom I could imitate, in a vocation open to women.

Anne Pederson was always well prepared, an intelligent lover of poetry and of people. She dressed beautifully (I remember her red dress at Christmas coffees in her apartment). She served exquisite cookies and the only coffee I thought good enough to drink. But most important, she was a superb teacher of literature, a friend, and mentor to many generations of Augsburg students. She was a person who lived her Christian vocation. Miss P., as we affectionately referred to her (but not in her presence), was a model of precision in speech and walk, yet her warm concern for everyone, from elderly faculty in need of a word of encouragement or humor, to tiny faculty children for whom she had a special charm, was unforgettable. Very few of my female friends and colleagues have been fortunate enough to know women teachers and professors with whom to identify.

It was from my parents that I learned the principle of seeking God's will. Then the example of women like Anne Pederson prepared me for life as a Christian professional. I didn't need to conform to the stereotypes for women in twentieth-century America.

The renewal of the women's movement in the late 1960s brought me to question more deeply what our society and the church have done, and continue to do, to keep women from achieving their full potential under God. I was already a firm believer in the right of women to attempt, and in their ability to achieve, as much as men in almost every area of life. Through the women's movement I became aware that I was limiting that right and ability to women who chose to remain single. For years I unthinkingly accepted the idea that if a woman got married she knowledgeably and willingly cut herself off from a variety of career possibilities, and from opportunities to say something about how and where her life would be lived. Finally, it dawned on me that no one says "When Greg and Jill get married, I wonder if Greg will keep on working." Yet that question is almost always asked about a woman with marriage plans.

Once I understood the ridiculous nature of that assumption about women and work, I was free to reconsider the importance of day-care facilities for children. I had always thought that those who chose to have children should be expected to take care of them. I had none, and therefore it was not a proper concern of mine or, I thought, of the institutions of which I was a part. But the women's movement taught me that alternatives to individual home care must be provided. Otherwise, there is no way for most women to be relieved of the almost total responsibility for child care at home which characterizes our society.

I became involved in the work of the Caucus on Women's Rights at the State University of New York in the early seventies. That brought me into contact with a wider range of women (and a few men) concerned about issues such as sexist language in the University motto, discrimination in retirement benefits, and the need for women's studies courses. (It took awhile to convince me of a fundamental need for research and teaching that focus on the neglected half of the human race.) I have never been part of an organized C-R (consciousness-raising) group, but I have been taught by friends, experience, and feminist readings.

My friends in the women's movement often called on me as the "house Christian" when they received a request to speak about women's liberation at church group meetings. I was the only feminist they knew who was also a Christian—or a member of any religious group, for that matter. The cleavage between the secular women's movement and the church is due to a variety of causes, and certainly some blame can be attributed to each side.

The principles of full equality and personhood for individuals of both sexes are found so clearly in the words and examples of Christ. But the record of the church through the centuries is abominable when it comes to the position of women in society and church. How can a liberated woman come to know Christ the Liberator through such an oppressive institution as the church? The church has committed the sin of omission in failing to preach the message of full liberation for all people. We must *(a)* make nonbelieving feminists aware of the heritage of full personhood found in the gospel and *(b)* make believers aware of the insights that the women's movement has provided for all of us in today's world.

Fermentation within me of these discoveries made me question one Sunday morning why a visiting female missionary was asked merely to give a greeting from the pulpit, whereas visiting male missionaries gave sermons. (Five years later we have had at least one female speaker give the morning message in our church.) I immediately began to compose in my mind an essay that I titled "Second-Class Citizenship in the Kingdom of God." Since I was on sabbatical leave, I decided to take time from my research to write the article, which I sent to *Christianity Today.*

Looking back on it now, I am chagrined at the tentativeness of portions of that article. I brought out the way the church had emphasized Scripture portions with seemingly negative statements about women's participation, but had overlooked the many biblical indications of women in full ministry. My article, viewed as quite radical by some of the magazine staff, was returned with a suggestion that it needed more biblical references. In the good old Protestant tradition, I went back to the Scriptures—and the more I read, the more I compared, the more I studied the verses, the more I became convinced that the church had emphasized only those sentences from Paul's writings that seemed to *limit* the position of women in the church. Almost no attention had been given to the *range* of Paul's statements about women in the church—nor to his own practice as an apostle. After all, he commended Phoebe, was taught by Priscilla, and formulated the magnificent statement of Galatians 3:28. That verse immediately became my personal text just as it belongs to all women who know the Scriptures.

I sent the manuscript back to *Christianity Today* with additions, and after some delay and considerable debate among the editorial staff, I received word that my article would be published. I was pleased that an evangelical periodical was willing to open the question, even with some misgivings. Interestingly, an article by Nancy Hardesty, dealing with the same issues more comprehensively, appeared the same month in *Eternity* magazine. Ms. Hardesty's piece opened up a whole range of possibilities concerning the position of women in society, in the church, and in marriage; its long-range effects are just beginning to be felt in an organized way in evangelical churches.

I thank God for the way in which the Holy Spirit has been

working to bring women in many parts of the country to recognize the importance of full emancipation for Christian women in church and society. The formation of the Evangelical Women's Caucus and its continuing life are testimonies to the blessing of God upon the church in this crucial way. The concerns of feminism and Christianity are inextricably linked in my own life and motivation, and I pray that the Christian church and the women's movement, alienated from each other as they so often appear to be now, may come to know the oneness of full liberation through the perfect Person, Jesus Christ.

Chapter Nine

Anne Eggebroten

IT'S NOT EASY to be a feminist in the church. I clearly remember the first time I hinted anything to other Christians about my new, uncertain ideas. As a senior in college, I was standing on the steps outside the library on a warm spring day, talking with two other Inter-Varsity leaders, both male. I don't remember what I said—perhaps I suggested electing a woman president of our I-V chapter, or perhaps I mentioned that certain verses about women in 1 Corinthians had been bothering me. But suddenly a glass wall fell between me and them. Their embarrassed silence and their loving grins told me, "We are loving your soul, but it's an effort." They no longer heard my words or had anything to say to me. I had become a clown or a fanatic to be observed with mild amusement.

Later I learned to guard my words, to withhold part of who I was until I was sure I would be accepted. Still later I learned that God accepts me. But even today I tremble as I feel that wall slide between me and another Christian.

When I was a sophomore in high school in 1963, I was un-

Anne Eggebroten is presently working on a doctoral dissertation on women in the church in the middle ages, at the University of California (Berkeley). Now living with her husband John Arthur in Concord, California, she was a founding member of the Evangelical Women's Caucus and has served on its national committee.

aware that I would ever become a feminist. I had recently become a Christian, through the ministry of the First Presbyterian Church of Bakersfield, California, where my mother had sent me both to gain some religious training and to develop a social life. We were new to the community, and to my mother's distress I spent more time studying and reading books than making friends. She dropped me off at Sunday night youth group and sent me on retreats, hoping I would form friendships and become normally socialized.

When my socialization at church resulted in an earnest conversion to Jesus Christ, my mother took it in stride: "You'll grow out of it, dear." The ironic thing was that my trust in Jesus as Lord and Savior made me vulnerable to a socialization more profound than my mother expected. I learned, for example, that in Christian marriages the husband rules the wife. I accepted it, though I knew that in our home such a thing would have been impossible. My father watched television, read newspapers, went to work, and drank beer; he was definitely not interested in ruling either Mother or the household.

My mother cooked, cleaned, sewed, baked, and supervised us kids in her spare time from teaching nursing at Bakersfield Junior College. As the oldest child of four, I filled the gaps in her management. If anyone ruled the household, I probably did. At any rate, I had had enough ironing, dishwashing, and child care at an early age to convince me that I didn't want to be a housewife. Some time along in my late high school and early college years I began proclaiming that I would never get married. I would be smarter than my mother. Marriage meant drudgery and, for a Christian, submission to one's husband. That was not the life for me.

Despite my verbal rebellion, no one could have discovered from my behavior that I had any misgivings about marriage. I endured a crush on the most popular boy at church and saved the dime he once lent me to make a phone call. I longed for dates, and I energetically observed all the customs appropriate to my half of humanity. I began wearing eye shadow and mascara and lipstick, and did my hair up on rollers every night. I manicured and painted my fingernails, which persisted in growing flat and soft. I would encourage my mother to wear nail polish, too, but she would laugh and say that that was for the young and foolish.

After my first couple of dates, the theory of dating puzzled me. I wondered in a letter to my grandparents why boys wasted their money on girls. "I wouldn't if I were a boy," I wrote. "I'd just as soon watch two movies with the amount of money I'd have to spend to watch one with a girl. However, I happen to be on the receiving end of the deal so I'm open to games and movies and the works."

One of my first real dates was to a Valentine's dance with a boy I didn't much like. But the status of going to a formal dance made it worthwhile. That dance was the occasion of one of the most bitter battles I ever had with my mother. She wanted me to buy a new dress for the event. I generally avoided shopping and resisted new clothes, partly because they were so important to my mother and partly because of the Bible passage about the lilies of the field, which made me think that preoccupation with clothes was wrong. At any rate, I didn't like to have my mother and the shop attendants fussing over me. On this occasion Mother hauled me down to the fanciest store in town and had me trying on dresses in utter misery. I was zipped and unzipped, scrutinized, and forced to comment on the dresses I despised. My mother attacked my glum demeanor with sharp remarks out of the hearing of the saleslady: "Now look here. Any other girl would be grateful." "Shape up. You ought to be ashamed of yourself acting like this." Finally I burst out crying. I stood in front of the mirrors in a black velvet jumper and silky white blouse, while the tears rolled down my cheeks. There was a big, floppy white bow at the neck of the blouse, coming down over the top of the jumper. "I don't know what's wrong with her, a daughter who cries when you try to buy her a dress," said my mother. Undaunted, she ordered purchase of the jumper, blouse, black patent leather heels, and a black patent leather purse. I wore them to the Valentine's dance.

Besides my goal of social acceptance at sweet sixteen, my main preoccupation was to get into a good university, earn a graduate degree, and start some career. The contradictions I lived never bothered me. I worked toward a career, but wanted a boyfriend; I didn't expect marriage, but anticipated wifely submission in marriage. My academic ambition came from my father, who would scrutinize my exams and essays from school and say "What about this *B?*" or "This part here is not very good." He certainly never set lower goals for his daughters than for his sons. He had interrupted his education for World War II and never completed college, and we all knew from him and my mother that we would go to college and have careers of some kind.

My mother had graduated from the University of Colorado and worked as a public health nurse from my earliest memories. When I was in fifth and sixth grades, she earned a master's degree in public health nursing, and after that taught nursing in college. There is a picture of us taken when she graduated: her in mortar board, tassle, and gown, with four children ranging down to age three. I learned stamina and emotional strength from my mother. She held the family together through times when my father was depressed and, for one year, unemployed. We would make it somehow, I knew from her. I was proud that she shared with me family worries, her experiences and problems at work, and even her fear of another pregnancy. She also taught me that you need a master's degree (at least) in order to have more freedom and authority in your work.

One incident disturbed me somewhat during my senior year of high school. A woman replaced my regular physics teacher for the last few months of the year, just after I had learned that I was accepted at Stanford University. With the doors of that glorious temple of knowledge opening to me, God's plan for my life seemed to be an unending stream of achievement and honor. "Oh, how nice," my physics teacher said, upon hearing of my admission. "I went to Stanford, too." "You did?" I asked incredulously. She worked part-time as a substitute science teacher and lived in Bakersfield with her husband, also a Stanford alumnus, and several children. That was definitely not my idea of the lofty future a Stanford graduate should have. I tucked the information away and assured myself that it would not happen to me.

Nevertheless, once at college, I doubled in two weeks the number of dates I had gone on in my life. The "ratio" meant that women were a small minority at Stanford, so I enjoyed concerts, free dinners, and a standard of living above my poor scholarship status. I also learned that boys expect something in return for their money, at the very least a kiss, but the arrangement still seemed like a bargain to me. Study was squeezed in on the side. I never connected dating to marriage at all. The one time marriage became other than a remote possibility, I ended the relationship. My high school boyfriend, after driving a thousand miles to see me at Christmas of my freshman year, had talked of how his best friend had just gotten married to a nurse who was going to work to put him through college. That was scary. I told him goodbye.

In my junior year of college I first heard about "women's liberation" and met John Arthur. When John first asked me out, I turned him down in order to sit home all night vainly hoping a guy I had liked in my freshman year might call me up. It was six months before my future husband got up enough courage to ask me out again.

There were a lot of jokes in our dorm room that year about the women's liberation movement, which had just surfaced in the media. Everyone thought the bra-burning (which never took place) was pretty funny. In a boisterous way I began saying, "Yes, I'm for 'women's lib' " amid the banter of three roommates and the friends and boyfriends that came and went. I didn't know what I meant, but I instinctively knew my allegiance was with it. When John pointed out to me on a camping trip that he liked me just as well—even better—without eye makeup, I was amazed. I stopped wearing it and thought I was a real "women's libber."

Throughout my senior year, I continued giving lip service to women's liberation and becoming more attached to John. It was apparent, however, that the dichotomies of my life were building toward a crisis. On the one hand, I was planning to go to graduate school and pursue a career. On the other hand, marriage was starting to become an actual possibility. I knew I had to choose between these two options: a career, or marriage with a side-dish of career.

The way my mother combined career and family, her family always came first. She quit her jobs when my father was transferred, she passed up professional meetings, and she squeezed graduate school in on the side. Though she regretted not having earned a Ph.D., having children was her main goal and joy in life—as she always reminded me. I dimly realized that my parents expected me to put both career first and marriage first. They had sacrificed to send me to a good college, but my mother would say, only half-jokingly, "Well, we're just sending you there to find a husband."

On graduation day I walked around with my diploma in one hand and John in the other. I savored my success in both realms, the academic and the social. Somehow I would be able to have my cake and eat it, too. The bliss of that day was untouched by the following facts: John was about to start a job in Boston. I was going to start graduate school at UC Berkeley in the fall. John was not a Christian. I would never marry a non-Christian.

We seemed to be going our separate ways, until one day in late September John asked Jesus Christ into his life. That was a big surprise to me. Suddenly the bulwark between me and marriage had collapsed.

It was a miserable fall. Though I liked having my own studio apartment in Berkeley, I missed John very much. The three married couples in the building were always trooping in and out by twos to play tennis or go out to dinner, and their cozy private existence grated on me. The women were putting their husbands through seminary, while not planning any careers of their own. Although intelligent and educated, they were content with most of the "female roles" such as cooking, and two of them were eager to have children. Most of all, I despised the dependence the husbands and wives had upon each other.

I began to take being a feminist seriously and decided to join the National Organization for Women, but since I was working my way through graduate school, I had no time to become active in it. Nor did I have time to read the classic feminist texts; instead, I clipped newspaper articles on women's liberation and taped them all over one wall of my kitchen. From them I learned about equalitarian marriage, keeping one's own name, and the oppression of women.

Whether to marry was my constant preoccupation. One part of me longed for the emotional and physical intimacy; another part of me recoiled in horror at becoming a wife. I was convinced that if I married I would go through a complete metamorphosis into a nonperson. I was also very skeptical of the chances for two people preserving their love and communication; most marriages I had known were dead relationships preserved for social and economic reasons.

During spring vacation of that first year in graduate school, John visited me and we debated marriage for a week. I named conditions necessary: staying in California, keeping my own name, being equal partners, and writing a marriage contract. John was agreeable to that. With him and with all those guarantees, I thought there might be a reasonable chance for surviving and thriving in spite of marriage.

During the next fifteen months before the wedding, I tried to adjust to giving away my independence, but my frustration level increased. I looked through every book I could find on Christian marriage to discover whether they all held to submission of wives. They did. I worked at *Christianity Today* in Washington, D.C., for the second summer, wrote a review of marital and premarital advice books, and battled *CT's* policy that had women employees of all ranks cleaning the coffee pot and catering food to men. One day on my lunch break in Lafayette Park, my frustration exploded at a poor, demented man who frequently preached there on the need for men to keep wives obedient. He stood raving on a stool, with sandwich boards over his shoulder, buttons, beanies, and pamphlets. For some reason on that day I could neither ignore him nor be amused by him; suddenly I jumped up, walked over to him, and pushed him off his stool, to the cheers of onlookers.

Another crisis occurred about six months before the wedding when I began reading birth control information. I studied the percentages of success for the various methods and the percentages of women who died each year by each one, and concluded it was all unfair. John didn't have to read any of this; he could just wander in and go through the ceremony, while I had to study, endure a humiliating physical exam, and pick one of several bad alternatives for birth control. Late one night after trying to figure out my choice, I got very angry at the Creator who had set up the whole male-female system. Not only did marriage mean bucking social expectations, defying certain Bible verses, and losing my freedom, it meant signing up for physical pain and danger in either childbirth or the prevention

of childbirth. "It's not fair," I yelled, throwing things around
the room, crying, and finally going outside at two in the morning to sit on the little plot of grass in front of the apartment
building and fume at the stars and at the God who created
them.

As the catastrophic event approached, John and I began
working on the contract that we hoped would protect both
of us from the oppressive roles forced on wives and husbands.
Some of the fifteen points were: sharing housework and cooking
50–50, sharing decisions affecting both partners, sharing child
care equally if we had children, taking turns on deciding where
to live, taking vacations from each other, retaining our given
names, and having separate checking accounts. As we wrote
about these things, we discovered where our expectations of
marriage differed: two weeks before the wedding we had a
crisis over whether the contract should describe children as
"possible" or "probable." With some trepidation, I gave in to
John's "probable." The contract began to look rather frail to
me in the face of mothers, grandmothers, fathers, uncles, and
aunts all determined to march us through a traditional wedding
and into a proper marriage.

On June 3, 1972, I got married and spent the next year
holding my breath to see if I had turned into that monstrous
creature, a "wife." I hardly believed we were married, because
I was just the same and John was just the same. We kept irregular hours and even more irregular mealtimes. John cooked every other meal and took his turn on all the household chores.
He also looked for a job, while I studied for my classes and
worked part-time. At church we went to different adult education classes.

My main method of preserving my identity was keeping
my own name. There were no legal problems, and every one
we knew accepted it—except our immediate families. My
mother was strongly opposed to my crazy ideas and embarrassed in front of John's parents that I wouldn't take their name.
My father was even more opposed. As he put it, "Why don't
you just get divorced? You aren't married as long as you don't
take John's name." Five years later, our parents are more accepting of this decision.

Just when I was beginning to discover that I could indeed

exist as a wife and a student, as a Christian and a feminist, I ran head-on into the opposition of the church. As in high school, the strongest attempts at socialization to the normal female role came from Christians. The first were my aunt and uncle who had crossed the country to come to our wedding. Over a beef dinner, my uncle began quoting Genesis about the husband ruling over the wife. I had no answer to that, except that I couldn't go along with it. Later my aunt strongly encouraged me to attend a Basic Youth Conflicts seminar where I would be straightened out, and pressed on me *Fascinating Womanhood* by Helen Andelin. When I looked through the book, I was horrified. My Christian aunt had given me something that was not only non-Christian but actually heretical at many points. It said things like "Your husband is your king; worship him." I can quote the book only loosely, because a couple years ago I decided that that pink and white heresy had been on my shelves too long. I took it down, set a match to a few of the middle pages, watched them burn, and then threw it out.

The second attempt to guide me away from my error came from the associate pastor of my church. I was teaching a series of classes on sexual ethics for the church's college group when he and the seminarian working with the college group asked me to come into the minister's office and get acquainted. I went. I explained about keeping my own name and having a marriage based on an equalitarian rather than a hierarchical model. They both questioned me about how I could do this in light of the Bible's teaching that the husband is the head of the wife, etc. We looked at some passages, and I was unable to defend my actions biblically. All I could say was "I think I'm right and the Bible is wrong," an untenable position for an evangelical. My confidence dwindled to "Well, I don't have the question completely resolved. Right now I think God approves my equalitarian marriage, but maybe he will convince me of my error." I felt miserable just leaving open that possibility. I left feeling very guilty, very rebellious, very shaky.

I grew more defensive. I would either hide my views among Christians or angrily and aggressively argue them. People would shoot Bible verses at me, and I could say only "I don't agree with that, though I do accept the Bible as God's Word."

I was alienated from God and angry at him. If male domination
were his will either in the church or in the home, he was a
God whom I couldn't wholeheartedly serve. I didn't think it
was his will, but I could never be sure. I was suspicious of
him but still trying to keep up a relationship with him.

Then in September 1974, I bought a copy of *All We're Meant
to Be*, just published. I went to my study carrel in the English
department and opened to chapters eight and nine on husband-
wife relations. I read fearfully, expecting each minute to come
across the proviso that the husband should theoretically rule
over the wife, however equal their relationship worked out
in practice. But no—only sentence after sentence of realistic
advice and sensible ways of handling the biblical texts. By the
time I came across the quotation, "Each for the other, and
both for the Lord," a great burden was lifted off my shoulders.
I began crying. I cried for my anger and anxiety in the past.
I cried with relief and joy at being reconciled to God again,
a God who loved me and whom I could love with my whole
heart. It was like a conversion experience. It seemed that God
had had the book written for me alone. He cared about me
and my struggles, even when I thought I was farthest from
him.

Since then, most of my time has been devoted to sharing
with others what I have learned, both in my own church and
with Christian women in other churches. Because very few
men or women in my own church are open to Christian feminism, the most satisfying sharing has been with Christian sisters
in other churches who have experienced the same struggle I
have. My first taste of that sisterhood occurred when I wrote
to Letha Scanzoni and Nancy Hardesty soon after reading their
book. That fall I went to a meeting of Evangelicals for Social
Action in Chicago, where fifteen women decided to found the
Evangelical Women's Caucus (see Appendix 4). In the years
since that 1974 founding, many women have banded together
to change the sexism in our churches and to encourage other
evangelical women. I have put much of my time into building
a chapter of EWC in the San Francisco Bay area, a network
of women and resources. As each new woman discovers us,
it is heartwarming to hear the tale repeated: "I thought I

was alone in my discontent with women's roles in the church. . . . "

Other women around the country are organizing chapters of EWC, too. Progress is slow, "total women" abound, and sisterhood is not easy to learn. Yet, with the Holy Spirit working among us, and through shared resources, publicity, and strength in numbers, I believe we will have an impact for good on the evangelical church in North America.

Chapter Ten

Catherine Kroeger

JESUS SAID, "You will know the truth, and the truth will make
you free." It is Jesus who has broken down the middle wall
of partition between people. It is he in whom there is neither
male nor female. Throughout my life God has often nudged
me to become involved in a work of reconciliation, but as a
wife and mother I found myself too busy to respond. At the
same time, my experiences sharpened my sense of the need
to understand God's will for the feminine half of the human
race. I am now researching the language and context of the
New Testament teachings about women. Increasingly I see
that the project requires an old war horse, a veteran of the
fray. The perceptions that have so long eluded male scholars
are far more comprehensible to someone who has lived through
a great many vicissitudes common to women of all generations.

I was born in the midst of the roaring twenties into a family
that believed staunchly in equal treatment of boys and girls,
whether in education, athletics, or inheritance. Both of my
parents were dedicated to the principles of the Bible; and both

*Catherine Kroeger, at age 52, is pursuing classical studies at the University
of Minnesota and specializing in women in ancient religion. She is president
of the Minnesota School of Missions (the state's oldest ecumenical organization)
and is a trustee of Whitworth College. She and her husband Richard live in
St. Paul.*

tried in their own ways to inculcate those precepts into the lives of their children. My father, raised in the tradition of Channing and Emerson, instilled in me the knowledge that God loved all people alike, and that each human being must be treated as a person made in the image of God. Although he was president of two large corporations and a member of the Ninth District Federal Reserve Board, he gave time and courtesy to everyone with whom he came in contact. Both in his business and personal life, he insisted on the highest standard of ethics and integrity. My mother, descended from a long line of godly Presbyterians but led to a personal knowledge of Christ by a Dutch Reformed aunt, exposed us not only to the evangelical traditions of the past but also to significant contemporary leaders. In 1939, C. Stacey Woods (one of the pioneers of Inter-Varsity Christian Fellowship in the U.S.) first visited our home and introduced us to the concept of student witness on the secular campus.

Mother hired a governess to tutor us during periods of illness and during the summer vacations. In that way, I was able to enter college with advanced standing in both French and classical Greek. One young governess, a recent graduate of Northwestern Bible School, led me into an acceptance of Christ as Lord and Savior and to an assurance of my salvation. On a couple of occasions she sneaked me over to First Baptist Church in Minneapolis to hear the preaching of W. B. Riley and Gypsy Smith. She saw to it that I was well supplied with Christian literature and gospel tracts, which I usually strewed about with more zeal than good judgment.

My sisters and I were sent to an independent school for girls. The headmistress, a formidable and talented woman, sent most of her graduates east to college at one of the Big Seven. "We are a hard school," she said, "and you are fortunate to be able to attend a school such as this." We were given to understand that if much was given to us, much would one day be required of us in community leadership. During all the years that I was growing up I don't remember anyone implying that women were in any way inferior to men—with perhaps one exception.

Summers were spent in the old family house on Cape Cod, built in 1799 by one of our seafaring ancestors. We swam almost as soon as we could walk; and when we could swim well, we were allowed to sail. At first our activities were confined to the sheltered waters of Cape Cod Bay, but my brothers grew more adventurous. The first step up was a Wianno Senior, a wonderful boat for young people because it has 500 pounds of lead in the keel. The rumor persists that anyone who can capsize a Wianno Senior may claim a prize of one thousand dollars. (We still prize that old boat, and I don't worry when my children go out sailing in her.) But the day came when my brothers wanted to do deep-sea cruising, and my father ordered a 42-foot yawl. She was a lovely vessel, built for speed but safe for long jaunts. I have many happy memories of day cruises and overnight trips, but the longer cruises were exclusively for the boys.

When it came to the longer deep-sea races, my sisters and I resented the discrimination. As we saw the shiny trophies coming home, we wanted desperately to share in the excitement and to be part of the crew: why weren't we as good as the boys? The boys pointed out that we lacked speed and precision. One cannot waste time with clumsy movements in a close race. My brother could jibe a spinnaker in less than 60 seconds. Could we match that? We drilled, and we drilled. But where was our strength to handle the heavy canvas with split-second timing? I recall the pathetic effort my sister and I made to demonstrate that the two of us were at least as strong as one boy. We each seized one end of a hand exerciser and tried fruitlessly to bring the ends together. Even with two of us pushing, the wretched thing wouldn't close; and my brother could with one hand manipulate it effortlessly and endlessly. More dispassionately, our parents pointed out that the "proprieties" simply didn't permit girls to participate in a race of several days' duration. In return we were given a virtual monopoly on horseback riding in the family.

My mother had a strong interest in Wheaton College and I was anxious to study in a Christian environment, but the headmistress had other ideas. I was accepted by both Bryn Mawr and Vassar, and in the end my parents shipped me off to Bryn Mawr. I was disappointed—but hopeful that a student Christian witness might be established there; in the first week I was visited by two IVCF staff members. I attended IVCF conferences and monthly area meetings in Philadelphia. I was impressed by the coherent answers given to questions being raised on secular campuses about the supposed discrepancies in the Bible. It became clear to me that the Bible could be trusted, but that diligent evangelical scholarship was still needed to resolve some of the apparent difficulties. There were answers if we would persist in looking for them.

One day an old friend from the Cape came to visit in the Philadelphia area. She was Harriet Hall, the granddaughter of A. J. Gordon, founder of Gordon College and Seminary, and associate of Dwight L. Moody. Her mother was Roberta Gordon Hall, who ran a gospel mission in Fitchburg, Massachusetts; her uncle, Ernest Gordon, wrote for the *Sunday-School Times*. Knowing that her mother enjoyed an effective ministry, I confided to her my perplexity about biblical views of the status of women. I was being educated to assume a position of leadership, yet I was aware of passages in the Bible that seemed to point in a different direction. She told me of the studies of Katherine Bushnell, who had wrestled with that problem, and lent me a copy of Bushnell's *God's Word to Women*— a great boon. The work had been published privately in 1919 and was difficult to obtain,[1] although it drew strong support from the *Sunday-School Times*. I was surprised at some of Bushnell's translations, but reference to the Greek text showed me the validity of many of her claims. The Hebrew was beyond me. The book issued a clear call for female translators and scholars if there was ever to be a reconciliation of the "anti-woman passages" with the biblical record of God's use of significant female leadership. I heard that call, but I was headed for the mission field. I figured that "women" would have to wait.

A year after I graduated from Bryn Mawr, I entered Yale School of Nursing to prepare myself for the mission field. I had spent the intervening year doing graduate work in English and Greek at the University of Minnesota, a course considerably more congenial to me than the physiology and organic chemistry in which I now toiled. During the year in Minnesota, I had served as a volunteer staff person for IVCF: and so I shortly found my way to the Yale IVCF chapter. It was there that I met my future husband, the president of the group. He was

hopeful of entering a new seminary on the west coast, an institution that would combine academic excellence with evangelical commitment. He seemed headed for the ministry, and I
was definitely bound for the deserts of Arabia, a goat's hair
tent, and life as a single missionary. Following his graduation,
he too felt called to the mission field; in the fall he left for
Fuller Seminary. My lassitude on the hospital wards at first
was taken for lovesickness, but presently it became apparent
that I had contracted a severe case of infectious hepatitis from
a patient. I was sent home to Minnesota and took nearly a
year to recuperate, after which we were married. I had been
able to continue a few more courses in English and Greek
and wrote my last exam the day before the wedding. While
my husband completed seminary, I worked and attended a
few classes taught by leading evangelicals like Wilbur Smith,
Dan Fuller, Carl Henry, George Ladd, Everett Harrison,
E. J. Carnell, and Harold Lindsell. I knew that I was in the
presence of superior scholarship and earnest spiritual endeavor.
Oswald Chambers had coined the phrase, "My Utmost for His
Highest," which seemed to me worthy of adoption as a life
slogan.

After my husband graduated and I gave birth to our first
child, we were accepted as candidates of the Sudan Interior
Mission and told that it would probably take a year for the
visas. Dick accepted a temporary pastorate in North Dakota,
serving three Presbyterian churches. At first we had no running
water, but in six months' time our kindly parishioners had supplied us with all the "conveniences"; the next winter a furnace
was installed just before the temperature plunged to −45°.
Our people were doing everything they could to let us know
they loved us and wanted us to stay. The SIM director came
to survey our work and said, "The field is the world. Frankly,
it would be harder to get someone to replace you here than
in Africa. Why don't you stay for a year?" The next year brought
another pregnancy complicated by a bout of infectious mono-
nucleosis. By then it was decided that I was not a good health
risk for the Sudan, especially as I was Rh negative and there
were no facilities to transfuse a baby.

North Dakota was itself a mission field and a proving ground.
The nearest medical facility was across the border in Canada;

it was there that I parted with my appendix on a homemade operating table in an old house that was being remodeled as a hospital. The doctor had advised that the drive over rough roads to more adequate facilities might result in a rupture of the appendix. Our prairie pastorate lengthened into four years; but the fifty-mile circuit over unpaved roads (often in blizzard conditions), three midweek prayer services, and three youth meetings were beginning to take their toll. Regretfully, we left for a parish in St. Paul. We had learned much from those wonderful communities where everyone had to pull together to survive the exigencies of nature. The women proved their worth a thousand times over, and no one questioned their equality with men.

By then I had three children under five years of age. Sometimes I would wonder if the day would ever come when I could minister to their heads instead of their bottoms! Besides the church work, my husband was asked to do chaplaincy service at a local detention home; there we came to see the desperate need for foster homes for delinquent girls. Christ said, "I was a stranger, and ye took me in" (Matt. 25:35, KJV) and "Whoso shall receive one such little child in my name receiveth me" (Matt. 18:5, KJV). Didn't that also apply to teen-age girls? I soon discovered that to receive unfortunate individuals into one's home runs counter to the stereotype of the model Christian wife. "Why disrupt the pastor's home like that?" The biblical picture of a home would never appear in *Better Homes and Gardens* for, like the church, it is to be an instrument of ministry. I believe that God gives us a front door through which to welcome those in need—and a dining room table on which to feed them.

When the social worker rang the doorbell, bringing the first girl to our home (she had just been released from a psychiatric ward), my knees shook so that I could hardly answer the door. The arrangement was to be temporary, only until there was an opening at an adolescent treatment facility.

Many foster children later, I can say that I don't believe we are ever adequate. We can only lay hold on God and trust him to work through us in the lives of needy young people. That first girl was returned to our home after she ran away from the treatment center, and she remained with us until

she was eighteen. Over the years we have had to cope with
shoplifting, lying, drunkenness, prostitution, venereal disease,
and homosexuality. A boy, we were told, will vent his hostility
in burglary and other outward acts of aggression, but a girl
will vent her hostility in acts directed against herself. Although
each of our girls came to trust Christ as Savior, none of them
really came to like or respect herself. In despair, I worked
on a committee to initiate group homes for problem girls in
our county. Although there are now a number of such homes,
many of them Christian, I see that they have not entirely met
the need. As I turned increasingly to the Bible, I saw that
those with low self-esteem must understand God's pattern: "in
his own image . . . male and female created he them" (Gen.
1:27, KJV).

When our sons reached their teens, our foster children became boys, usually foreign students or missionary children.
When people ask me how many children I have, I answer
that I'm not quite sure. I've lost track. Currently we have a
Laotian refugee, age fifteen; and a Norwegian exchange student, age nineteen.

As I lay in the recovery room after the birth of my fourth
child, I became aware of someone sobbing in the next cubicle.
"You'd better get in there," I told the nurse, "it sounds as
though she's about to deliver."

"It's all right," came the answer. "She already has."

"Well, then, you'd better get the doctor. Something must
be wrong."

"The doctor is with her, and so are her parents."

The sobbing continued unabated for a long time, inter-
spersed with exclamations, "I'm sorry, oh, I'm sorry!"

"Isn't she married?" I inquired when next the nurse appeared.

"I don't think so," she replied and promptly disappeared.

By now, thoroughly roused, I lost patience with the medical
staff. "Hey, you over there," I called, "pull back the curtain!"
A thin little hand appeared at the edge of the curtain and
pulled it back. There appeared a young tousled girl in the
bed and behind her the round, frightened eyes of her mother.
The parents had had no idea that she was pregnant and had

brought her to the hospital with what they supposed to be appendicitis. The startled family physician had commandeered my obstetrician to deliver a baby girl three months prematurely. "My name is Cathie," I volunteered, "What's yours?"

The sobs stopped, and the conversation began. The parents promptly left, and I was on my own. At first I wondered in panic what a thirty-seven-year-old married woman might with propriety discuss with a sixteen-year-old girl, but we got along beautifully once I gave up on delicacy and decorum. We had shared a common experience of motherhood that night. The staff made no effort to remove either of us from the recovery room for the next few hours, and we talked about many things. I tried to share with her God's forgiving and redeeming love, but then I didn't know that he had said "Now will I cry like a travailing woman" (Isa. 42:14, KJV) and "As one whom his mother comforteth, so will I comfort you" (Isa. 66:13, KJV).

A pastor's wife has a special vantage point from which to make observations on human nature. She copes not only with those who seek to monopolize too much of her husband's time but also with those who fear to approach the pastor at all and so end up consulting his wife. So often the problems they bring are distinctively those of women; so much more biblical insight is needed. Does the Bible *really* teach that women are to be doormats rather than full-orbed human beings? Why do some fundamentalists deny to women the rights of decision making, self-determination, and independent action? Why does the Scripture tell wives to "be subject" rather than to "obey" as it commands children and slaves? What is the difference in the two Greek verbs?

I recall the day that the Ladies' Aid finally left the manse, and I sat down to nurse my starving infant whose patience had been sorely tried. A woman returned to the house with her husband and they began to pour forth their grief and concern over a wayward daughter. I was writhing with embarrassment, but a nursing mother bothered them not one whit. They wanted loving ministry, not prudery—so I wracked my brain to find how my education might in any way have prepared me to help in so sordid a situation. The Holy Spirit gave me the words to say.

As our church people inaugurated an increasing number of
Bible study groups in their neighborhoods and places of business, my husband returned to school in order to gain more
biblical training. People were hungry for a deeper knowledge
of the Word of God, and he wanted to give it to them. In
the midst of his advanced studies, I began to have gynecological
problems and phoned the doctor. In all probability I was pregnant again, he told me, but the odds of carrying to full term
were not good. What did parents in their forties do? Did we
dare to risk bringing a mongoloid child into the world? Was
it right to give a child such elderly parents? Was it worth all
the morning sickness and misery if there was so little chance
of a baby anyway? I had experienced considerable difficulty
in carrying my other pregnancies and had lost several of them
despite every effort to keep them. As we prayed, we came
to understand that God's wisdom was higher than ours and
his answers better. We would do nothing to interfere with
the pregnancy nor to retain it: we would leave the matter in
God's hands. Months later God blessed us with another healthy
child. In answer to the jeers of even our Christian friends,
my husband dubbed us "Abraham and Sarah"; I thought of
the miracle of Sarah's motherhood—and the minor miracle I
now needed: strength to chase a toddler. In the ten years since,
I was given not only the strength but have become a distance
swimmer, a Red Cross water safety instructor, and am currently
taking a course in water polo.

After twenty years of always having a preschooler at home,
I saw our youngest child enter first grade. Then it was time
for me, too, to go back to school. I applied to the classics department of the University of Minnesota because I wanted to understand the language and the background in which the apostle
Paul had written his difficult teachings about women. He had
used rare Greek words, ones used in the New Testament only
in reference to women, and I wanted to study their occurrence
in other classical writings. That might shed light on the biblical
usage. I needed to understand the sociological, religious, and
sexual conditions of ancient women before they came to Christ.
Why was Priscilla allowed to teach if the women of Ephesus
were not? Wasn't that another dichotomy of Scripture that

needed to be researched conscientiously and painstakingly, as
Bushnell had said? I had always supposed that younger women
would take up the challenge, but I was tired of waiting. So,
shortly after my forty-ninth birthday, I was readmitted to graduate school. Many women have shared with me their terror
in going back to school, but I think perhaps I was most terrified
of all. Sometimes I wondered whether I had forgotten everything I had learned thirty years before, or whether I had never
really learned it in the first place. But the Lord helps my infir-
mities, and little by little the picture of his grace in the lives
of women grows.

I visited Yale for parents' weekend during my son's senior
year and discovered in the classics library new light on the
phrase, "I forbid a woman to teach or usurp authority." A dis-
tinctly different translation was possible.[2] I was so excited that
I almost cartwheeled back to my son's dormitory. My children
still at home support their mother's efforts to do research with
one hand in the dishpan and the other in the classroom. My
husband has become increasingly aware that my research of
biblical backgrounds and his in the Bible itself are strongly
correlated. When he requested permission to write his Ph.D.
dissertation on Paul's view of women in 1 Corinthians 11, he
was categorically refused on the grounds that the women question was already overworked and that he misunderstood the
passage totally if he thought it contained positive support for
women. We see no fundamental inconsistency in the biblical
precepts concerning women, but rather a drastic lack of eluci-
dating scholarship.

Every Saturday my kitchen abounds in homemade bread;
but it is all gone by Monday morning, and again my desk is
a jumble of classical, *koine*, patristic, and Byzantine Greek,
of church fathers and ancient courtesans, Roman marriage laws
and Christian heroines, with the children's mislaid homework
mixed in. My husband is thinking seriously of retiring from
the active ministry in order to bring to the project his skills
and New Testament scholarship. "And are not two better than
one?"

How can one understand Psalm 23 apart from knowledge
of Palestinian shepherd life, and how can one understand the

directives toward women apart from a knowledge of the world
in which they were given? [3]

NOTES

1. *God's Word to Women* by Katherine C. Bushnell has been privately
printed by Ray B. Munson (Box 52, North Collins, N.Y. 14111) and is available
for $5 plus postage, prepaid. A much abridged edition of Bushnell's work,
The Magna Carta of Women, the work of Jessie Penn-Lewis, has been published
by Bethany Fellowship (1975).
2. This resulted in "Isn't It Time for a New Look at 1 Timothy 2:12?" a
paper prepared for the Twin Cities Presbytery.
3. As this book goes to press, two articles by Catherine and Richard Kroeger
have been accepted for publication in the *Reformed Journal:* "Paul and the
Sexual Identity Crisis" (1 Cor. 11:1–15) and "Pandemonium and Silence at
Corinth" (1 Cor. 14:34–35).

Chapter Eleven

Katie Funk
Wiebe

MY HUSBAND WALTER died of a rare disease on November 17, 1962. I was thirty-eight years old, and we had four children. To me, his death meant being ceremoniously ushered out of the life I'd known and enjoyed—into a completely new way of living. At first this new way seemed to be a continual stepping down and away from life, an emptying and a vast emptiness. A humiliation. *Now I am a widow,* I thought to myself. The typical poor widow of every old novel I've ever read. Now people bring me flour and castoff clothing. Perhaps I'll be expected to take in washing and scrub floors to support my children.

Every morning when I awoke I faced a new batch of tasks to look after, some of which I knew something about, others totally new. The brakes of the car needed repair, one of the children needed new shoes, another six letters had to be written, the landlord had to be reminded of the leaking faucet. Inside I had little or no feeling, except for general nausea at the sight of food and the overwhelming sensation, "This can't

Katie Funk Wiebe is a prolific writer, the author of Alone: A Widow's Search for Joy *(Tyndale House, 1976), from which this chapter is excerpted, and* Day of Disaster *(Herald Press, 1976). For several years she was an editorial assistant at the Mennonite Brethren Publishing House. Since 1967 she has served as assistant professor of English at Tabor College (Hillsboro, Kansas.)*

go on. My circumstances have finally become too much for God and for me."

My widowhood brought home to me in the most convincing way imaginable what I had begun to suspect as a wife: that women are treated as second-class citizens in the church as well as in the world. Theoretically we may be joint-heirs with men in the freedom that Christ brings, but in practice we are bound by centuries-old prejudices passed on by the male leadership of the church.

I had grown up in a particularly free community. Our little village in northern Saskatchewan was composed of every nationality and creed: Russian, Doukhobor, English, Scottish, Irish, French, Ukranian, Indian, Polish, German.

The community was not especially religious, but a few churches stood as sentinels at the corners of the town, keeping evil at bay—a Roman Catholic church with a fairly large parish and a seven-thirty bell calling its parishioners to morning mass; a United Church of Canada with a good-sized Sunday school, a dwindling Ladies Aid, and a meager attendance at other services; an Anglican church in which a visiting minister held services once a month; a Russian Baptist church with exuberant singing.

Christianity was important in my family. Since churchgoing was needed for respectable living, and since our own denomination wasn't represented in the community, we lived a double life. Contact with our church twenty miles away across the Saskatchewan River was spasmodic because of the weather and road conditions—no cars traveled in winter and we had no horse and sleigh. So in summer we were Mennonite Brethren; in winter Mother and Dad were Russian Baptist—and we children, who couldn't understand Russian, were United Church.

My storekeeper father's ambitious goal for his four daughters and one son was to give us each sufficient education to make us self-supporting independent persons. As a new immigrant to Canada who had been unable to receive an education in the Mennonite colonies of the Ukraine in Russia, he valued education highly as the stepping stone away from manual labor to a freer life. My mother supported him in his goals for us.

Marriage was expected in a vague sense, but the passive home-maker role wasn't stressed.

By a strange set of circumstances I found myself living in a convalescent home shortly after I left high school to work in the city. Perhaps living so close to people who had lost their grip on life caused me to think seriously that summer. Life was busy, but it was dull. I had a job, but I couldn't call it a vocation. I called myself a Christian, but I wasn't a disciple.

One Saturday morning as I rummaged through some untidy shelves of old books and papers, I came upon a grubby-looking book of daily devotional readings. Any book was better than no book, so I took it to my room. The words of Scripture leaped from the page: " 'Ye shall be holy; for I am holy' [1 Pet. 1:16, ASV]. Continually restate to yourself what the purpose of your life is. The destined end of man is not happiness nor health, but holiness."

To find the right words for the right moment is an experience akin to discovering a gold mine. I stared at the words as ideas tore loose and raced in all directions within me. That day, my weak faltering faith received strength. My aimless feet were put on course. My ambitionless life was given a goal. A rebellious spirit yielded to the Master.

Very soon after that, I became an active member of a local youth group in the city where I was working. During World War II, "youth fellowships" of every nature and description were blossoming across the country. The will of God for our lives, Christ's love for all people, Christian fellowship, and Bible study became our passion. I read my Bible avidly to find out more about this exciting Christian way and in my newfound zeal spoke up openly in youth meetings.

My eager tongue and ambitious plans for the group soon got me elected president, not totally a surprise, for I had enjoyed being part of the action in my high school. Within a matter of weeks, though, some of my "young brethren," at the request of the pastor and church council, asked me to resign. Something about my shape and bodily functions made it impossible for me to continue in the office. Because God's glory was more important to me than youth group presidencies, I readily consented. Perhaps I had misunderstood God's will.

Only much later did I seriously wonder that if the Lord's work is important and a woman is the person best suited for the task, why isn't she allowed to do the work? I have since noticed that a man with little experience and enthusiasm for a work will often be chosen when better prepared and more interested women are left on the sidelines as a cheering section.

After several years of working as a legal secretary and two years in college, I married, expecting to spend the rest of my life safely isolated from society, secure in my husband's love, caring for my children and home. I never saw myself in any other role and never suspected I might be forced to seek one as a widow. I never saw myself other than as a contented wife and mother. Never middle-aged. Never alone.

Married life began for Walter and me as it does for so many other newlyweds, as a big glorious adventure of togetherness. Together we would conquer life and serve our God. That heady feeling of "winner take all" soon fled before the burden of cramped quarters, limited budgets, and lonely days, first as a student's wife and later as a young pastor's wife. We were faced with the added challenge of a low income and the fact that my husband wanted to complete his education, interrupted by the war. I took a deep breath and dived in, intent on becoming the best Christian homemaker possible.

Very soon I sensed a certain frustration and bitterness creeping in. As a single person I had become extremely interested in all aspects of the work of church and denomination. Working for awhile in a church college office as secretary, I had become familiar with all aspects of our programs. Now, all of that except children's work in the local church, the sewing society, and musical activities were off limits. My intellectual life had dwindled pathetically, so I returned to studying the Scriptures and other books. But I could find nothing to answer my uneasiness about myself as a *person*. The church seemed to address me only as a woman (who should ask no questions), not as a person (who happened to be female).

Only later did I realize that my uneasiness was part of a syndrome affecting women all over the nation—women between thirty and forty who had probably dropped out of school to marry, moved to the suburbs, had children; whose husbands moved into business or professions; and who one day found they had stopped growing in order to satisfy that one goal in life: to marry and have children. I was caught in the current of the rapid changes taking place regarding a woman's role in life. Betty Friedan didn't cause it; she merely drew attention to it in her book. Questions I'd been asking for years now demanded answers. Who really am I? Am I a person first or a woman first? Do I have to think of myself only in terms of the wife-and-mother roles in life I have to fill, much as I enjoy them?

In our small preacher-conscious church world, husbands were status symbols, and some women received their sense of importance and identity through the prominence of their preacher-husbands in church and conference work. Even my naive mind soon sensed that such an approach was a strange way of getting relevance out of life. Could I find sufficient meaning in life being the wife of the Rev. Walter Wiebe, a young minister, without making any specific contribution to life on my own? Must I live my life through him and the lives of my children? To do so wasn't unusual. My mother had had no other ambition in life.

What would happen if Walter died? Who would I be then? What would give meaning to my life as a widow? I felt guilty even questioning what seemed right: that a woman should find complete fulfillment in her role as wife and mother and never expect God to require anything more of her. She had found her sphere of service. Was I failing God by questioning traditional interpretations of the Word of God? Was I sinning by wanting to serve God with gifts I thought I had—in writing, for example? Was I actually only trying to wiggle out from under the authority of God's Word?

I had begun married life with the idea that it would be my whole life, so I kept myself busy at domestic tasks. I sewed all the children's clothes and my own, even coats at times. I gardened and canned up to 400 jars of fruit and vegetables each year. I learned a little about butchering. After psyching myself up with strong words of encouragement, I could even enter the henhouse, corner a young rooster, persuade him to lie still on the chopping block, and lop off his head—even though my heart pounded as wildly as his beheaded body once the head was gone.

I became an active church worker in Sunday school teaching, women's work, children's work. I helped my husband as his secretary. I enjoyed the creative challenge of many aspects of that work. I gave the church and my family everything I could, but I gave myself very little—because to listen to myself was to bring on feelings of guilt.

The harder I worked to fulfill the role of successful church woman, the more futile it seemed. I wanted desperately to serve God and do what the church taught regarding women. Yet there seemed to be an empty rhetoric there not substantiated by my own experience. I had some private conversations with a few women who, though they spoke publicly of being "happy in the Lord," were inwardly disquieted by the direction their lives were taking. I wondered why, if Christianity was an authentic option for women of the twentieth century, it didn't make them exciting, alive persons.

I became increasingly aware of the forces of society and church pushing my husband and myself in different directions, so unlike our college experience when we'd had common interests. We had worked together on the school newspaper and in other activities, side by side. Now we were members of the same church, but he had first-class citizenship and I second-class. He went to the policy-making meetings; I attended women's meetings and mission rallies. He helped make decisions; I served coffee. He studied the Word of God; I sewed and hunted for bargains in clothing and tracked down recipes and telephoned. It saddened me when sometimes the extent of our women's fellowship was to encourage each other to hang a Scripture verse above the kitchen sink: "I can't do much else for the Lord, but as I wash my dishes I can think nice thoughts." In the typical women's group, I could see no potential Catherine Booth or Mary Slessor or Florence Nightingale. Was embroidering tea towels and quilting really what God wanted of most women in this desperate age? Was there no legitimate purpose for education other than insurance against a husband's early death? What should a woman do with the longing within her to enjoy the craftsmanship of writing, painting, teaching, leading? I wondered. I agonized. Adding to the agony was the knowledge that women who found full satisfaction in cooking and cleaning couldn't understand the dilemma of their sisters like me. I was misunderstood.

I was looking for an identity that satisfied God's Word and fit the times in which we lived. Magazines were full of articles about the growing pains of women my age, but the church was silent. When I talked to men about the matter, some were immediately threatened and defensive, unready to yield position and make room for women in the church other than in traditional roles. If they did budge, it was frequently with an attitude of dispensing favors to the peons. Few women I spoke to at that time had the liberty to consider what seemed heresy. The Bible had sufficient texts that I should know my role, they said. So my answers had to come from elsewhere, not because I rejected the Bible but because the array of interpretations was more confusing than helpful.

Some of the first glimmers of light came from a combination of reading Scripture and other writings. I stumbled one day upon Christ's words, "Thou shalt love thy neighbor as thyself." I'd read those words hundreds of times, probably, but suddenly they took on new meaning. Love myself? Who had ever heard of such a thing? One was supposed to love others, but to love oneself? How did one do such a thing?

During my developing years I so often heard preaching about death to self: "He must increase, I must decrease." I went through young adulthood believing that it was scriptural to hate oneself, that it was important to die to self, to become a "nothing" so that Christ could become everything. "Self" and "life" became almost dirty words. A Christian had no right to think of self-actualization. I watched Christians struggling toward the goal of becoming "channels only," "instruments," and "meek, insignificant worms" like Jacob.

It is true that Scripture teaches death to sin and the carnal self, but it also teaches being alive to God. As I studied the Bible, particularly newer translations, I found that Christ said many things about self and the quality of a person's life on this earth. Paul assured the Ephesians that life has purpose. Christ talked about wholeness of personality and a full life. I began to doubt that a wormlike creature has a very significant or meaningful life. Christ intended his followers to make life itself their vocation while on earth and to use all the gifts he had given them in creative self-expression.

Any object, or life itself, becomes meaningful if it's worth something to someone. A Christian's life is worth a great deal to God. Didn't God love the world so much that he gave his Son for it? If he loves individuals that much, we have reason to love ourselves—at least as much as we love our neighbor. When we give our lives over to God, God gives us back our true selves to serve him. We become stewards of our personality. God doesn't return to us a shell or an empty husk of a body with the Holy Spirit rattling around inside. He gives each believer an individual personality, gifts, and talents sanctified by the Spirit.

Christ living in me—not in a worm—that was meaningful living. I had to learn to accept myself as God had made me and accepted me: first of all as a person. Mary at the feet of Jesus must have seen herself as a person, not as a woman whose role it was to serve the men a meal. Priscilla, Phoebe, and Dorcas seemed to do likewise. Maybe there was room for me in that group. Yet I knew that without present-day role models and supporting organizational structures in our conservative church, the way wouldn't be easy to fit into a nontraditional role.

I cherish the words of Dr. Marion Hilliard, a medical doctor, who before her early death did considerable writing about women's role and problems. "From the time a woman is born until she dies, she is not only a woman, but also a person." Unless she regards herself in this way, she will be "whatever the economy asks, or what the men think beautiful, or what the children want to make them happy. . . ."

Dietrich Bonhoeffer, the German theologian, wrote that God doesn't ask us to come to him in order to crush our identity and will. Yet to accept the traditional mold for women seemed to crush my own personhood. I simply wasn't prepared to spend my life embroidering as a way of serving God. I did that as a hobby. I needed to accept myself as I was, even though others might consider me strange if I chose reading over canning, and writing over quilting.

To accept myself meant accepting some of my secret urges and longings. As a high school student I had penciled to myself in a journal my desire to be a writer. In Jesus' parable, the man who failed to develop his talent was condemned to "outer darkness." His sin was failing to reach God's mark for him. The woman who was caught in adultery was told to "Go and sin no more." What a difference in punishment.

Somehow we have the idea that God's will for us will always be disagreeable and will require the breaking of our will to accept. Are anguish and misery prerequisites to doing the Lord's will? I am thankful that the newer books on the gifts of the Spirit point out that God has no desire to crush our creativity. He wants to help us fulfill our potential, whether we are wives, mothers, widows, or single. Doing so need not destroy family solidarity.

My first step was to set up a small table with my typewriter on it under the chimney corner of our parsonage. It became "Mom's desk." I was doing something pleasant, exciting, and profitable to me. I wrote a few news releases for a church periodical. I got back words of praise. I had begun a new life. I didn't expect other women to adopt *my* pattern of living, for I believe God leads each person individually, but now I could do the cooking and dusting more joyously.

While doing some research in church history, I read about a young woman in Manitoba in the 1870s, who, as a young wife with a good-sized family, five or six children, took a course in midwifery in a distant city at the suggestion of the church, and in the absence of a doctor in the area delivered over 700 babies during her lifetime. No harsh words were spoken against her because she gave her life to God as a "career woman" in addition to serving her family. Perhaps I longed for that kind of open encouragement from the church as I struggled with acknowledging my own gift. Yet I cannot blame the church, for, as fearfully as I, it too was moving through uncharted ground in regard to women's increasing demands for more living space.

My early writing attempts led to helping my husband in his work of editing a small periodical for youth workers in the church. I enjoyed the creative activity, and, as my husband became more active in other church duties, the editing became mostly my effort. When he suggested to the administrative committee that because I was doing most of the work and apparently quite successfully, I be appointed editor, their reaction was negative. They couldn't engage a woman as editor.

Again I became aware that the church doesn't fully reckon with its women as a spiritual force other than in Sunday school work with children, in the home, or in the church kitchen. For an overseas missionary, doors open a little crack. But women missionaries had mentioned to me repeatedly that though they carried heavy work loads, they were shut out of the decision-making meetings that covered their field of work. Frequently they had to get their information indirectly from a male missionary's wife.

For a time I wrote book reviews for a religious periodical when one of the regular reviewers couldn't keep up. I began writing a column for women in our denominational paper with the underlying assumption that my words might somehow help them live better lives as women of the home and church. Still, a troubling question was, why a "women's corner" at all in a church paper? The basic assumption seemed to be that women were very different creatures from men, requiring a different approach or a different interpretation of certain passages of Scripture. And one of the main differences seemed to be that they must be kept "in their place," whatever that meant. Women's service was usually determined by limitations rather than freedom.

I took a major step in my pilgrimage the day I recognized I had to write as a person to persons. If what I had to say was worthwhile, it shouldn't be pushed into a corner just for women. I decided to change the name of my column to "Viewpoint," fearfully, and against some opposition. I found I gained wider readership and a larger field of ideas to write about.

Some readers have sensed that over the years my viewpoints have changed on certain issues. That was inevitable as I continued to read and study and meet new experiences. To change one's attitude can be a difficult and painful procedure because it means honestly facing what is inside oneself. To change means being willing to follow new light without guilt about what others will say. To change means being willing to admit that even God doesn't always hold a man or woman to his original instructions to them. To change doesn't necessarily mean one must reject the past. One can affirm the good in the past and move on to the new.

The experience of widowhood probably caused the greatest change in my thinking. I had accepted as my role in life, as the will of God, that I should be a housewife and mother. God had put me there. I had liked my place. But suddenly I was forced to change my role. I was a widow, not a wife. I had to accept this truth: Faithfulness to God is more important than faithfulness to tradition, or to earlier maps one has made for one's life.

Chapter Twelve

Joyce Shutt

THIS IS A LOVE STORY, God's love story. I smile as I write, because I used to rant and rave about being sick and tired of God getting the credit when the going was good, but my catching the blame when things bombed. I'm still a little touchy about that. I don't see people as helpless pawns, but then I don't see them as all that competent, either.

My growing up was ordinary enough except I was a little luckier than a lot of kids. My parents reared us in an atmosphere of love, acceptance, financial security, high ethical standards, and the assurance that God is real even when we doubt and question. They taught us to work and play with gusto, and I eased into adulthood with many skills that have served me well. Too well, in fact. I became so adept at doing things that I had little patience with others who couldn't measure up. I believed that if you worked hard, did your best, followed the rules, prayed every night, went to church, and put others first, you'd live happily ever after.

Joyce Shutt, a graduate of Bluffton College (Ohio), is a master's in arts and religion candidate at Lutheran Theological Seminary, Gettysburg, Pennsylvania. She and her family live outside of Orrtanna on a fruit farm. A writer for various Mennonite publications, she is chairperson of the committee of ministers at the Fairfield Mennonite Church, and is active in many church and community organizations.

It doesn't always work that way. I found that out, however, only after meeting my Prince Charming and riding off into the sunset with him. Even though we worked hard, had four children, took in foster children, followed the rules, prayed every night, lived in the country, and went to church, one day we had to face facts: the sun had set on our romance.

In over twelve years of marriage, I had never refused my husband sexually or openly challenged his decisions. We disagreed often enough, but since both of us believed that the husband was the undisputed lord of the family, it was my duty to swallow my feelings and go along with his opinions. When I did try to exert myself or get my own way, I'd use manipulation, "martyring," or seductive methods. I took great pride in being a submissive Christian wife. Oblivious to reality because I was so wrapped up in my fantasy, I felt secure, loved, and in complete control. Imagine my shock when Earl said he no longer loved me.

I get into trouble here if I try to tell this as just my story. It simply doesn't come off. Something has happened to me that is both dramatic and beautiful. Just ask my family and friends. But I didn't make it happen alone. God touched my life. With the help of some very special people, he set me free.

Earl's confession never warranted my extreme reaction. But after thirty-five years of trying to please others, of living vicariously through their achievements and experiences, and of being a good little Christian, at some unconscious level I was looking for an excuse to change. Earl provided that. And so I found myself, as it were, standing naked before the burning eyes of my husband, my God, and myself. I couldn't stand it. I cracked up.

Then began a long process of reshaping my life around a new set of values, of becoming my own person. It started with therapy. It ended with God.

I hurt so that there were times when I literally couldn't breathe. I longed for numbness, the old anesthesia that comes from hard work, stifled emotion, and rigid self-control. But I seethed with such a backlog of unresolved feelings and raw emotion that nothing worked. I felt so vulnerable, defenseless, and empty that I'd try to hide behind a wall of anger that never quite held up. I often contemplated suicide, but I also developed the ability to step outside myself and to observe what I was doing. Sometimes I'd look so ridiculous to myself that I'd start laughing or crying right in the middle of a tirade.

All the skills and work habits that I'd acquired as a child carried me through many a day's crisis. I'd turn on my automatic pilot and somehow manage to cook supper, bathe the boys, shop for groceries, make a dress, or whatever. But with Earl it was different. He was the weak link in my armor. He knew my secrets. I could cope or relax around others, but with him I'd freeze up. Everything that I wasn't and wanted to be was focused in his person. I loved him, I hated him, I clung to him with a wild desperation I couldn't understand. One negative word or look from him and I'd go to pieces.

In many ways I was too smart and too successful for my own good. There were so many things I didn't want to face, but so many things I wanted to change (without pain, of course) that I'd come up against a hard place and I'd start maneuvering, looking for an easier way or someone else to blame. I'd even outwit, outthink, and outtalk my therapist.

I took everything Freud and his cronies said about women and their immature sexuality and turned it against myself. My head rebelled, but my gut believed. A woman could write, think, talk, cook, sew, care for children, sing, be affectionate, manage a business, etc., but when it came down to the fine line, she was only as good as her orgasms. It seemed hopeless.

It got so bad that I hated to go to bed at night. I'd tighten up just climbing the stairs. My sexual response (or lack of it) became the measure of my self-worth. I was so afraid of not feeling the right thing that I felt nothing. I'd panic when Earl touched me, terrified I'd fail, which inevitably I did. But oh, how I longed for closeness and love.

We were caught up in a vicious cycle that seemingly had no end. Our therapist recommended the "total woman" approach, but for me, sexual responsiveness involved more than a pretty nightgown, a five o'clock bubble bath, or a new place or position. A woman's responsiveness, I discovered, has more to do with how well she likes herself, with being at peace, and thus able to give from an overflowing wellspring of inner contentment.

And then I met a minister, a male chauvinist, who represented all I loved and hated in the society and church. Somehow he made it safe for me to fight my battles with God and the world. And fight I did. He used his flowery evangelical language and I swore like a truckdriver. He quoted Scriptures and I challenged his belief in divine inspiration. I'd make the most heretical statements and he never seemed shocked. He'd listen, process, and feed back my hysterical comments as serious and important insights. He cried over my poetry. He felt my pain. He helped me see myself as a whole person.

Each February I attended a week-long international meeting since I was on the literature committee of the Women's Missionary Association of the General Conference Mennonite Church. Things hadn't improved at home, and I arrived in Kansas one year with tears so close to the surface that my ever-present anger was my only defense. I'd been reading feminist literature, and I was defensive as all get out, mostly because I was aware of how vulnerable I was and how much I depended on others for approval, especially men.

Thus I was as shocked as anyone when I stood up in the middle of a session and shouted at the men, "You make me sick. You think that there is only one kind of person in the world: ordained men! Well, I've got news for you. There are a lot of people out there in the world. Most of them aren't ordained and many aren't even men!"

When no hole opened up in the floor for me to fall through, I ran sobbing from the room. I was still crying when the door opened and someone came toward me. "That was beautiful," he said. "We needed to hear that. Do you know that you have a gift for emotion? I hope that you will continue to share that with us in the future."

I couldn't believe my ears. One of the men I'd blasted, a pastor, prophet, poet, and writer was complimenting me on my childish outburst. "Don't be afraid of your feelings," he went on. "Not everyone feels as deeply as you do. Feelings are a gift, you know."

I apologized for my outburst to the women's missionary group, and even offered to resign. They refused. "We need you," one older woman said. "You have words for the feelings we also feel. We understand your struggle. It's our struggle, too."

Such acceptance and encouragement did more to help me

accept my humanness than twenty therapy sessions. Those people had no reason to accept me and yet they did. For the first time in my life I really felt that my emotional intensity was a strength, not a weakness, and that instead of trying to suppress it, I should try to find ways to use it constructively.

A few months later, I met that pastor again in Minneapolis when I attended a mass evangelism rally. I went scared, uptight, and feeling very much alone. He must have sensed how frightened I was, for he invited me to participate in his peace evangelism workshop. I was so grateful that I tagged along behind him like a puppy. When we began planning the antiwar demonstration, I relaxed; my struggles gave me some insights into human dynamics others did not yet have. "Whatever we do, we dare not attack the people who work at Honeywell Corporation. They are not bad people. War is the evil, not the people."

Our visit to Honeywell was my first experience in a peace deputation that involved personal evangelism. When one of the Honeywell men opened up and shared his anguish and struggle, I was so awed by his courage and depth of feeling that I went up to him. "I feel for you. Nothing seems to work out the easy way for me either."

As I sat and listened during the four days of talks and activities at the rally, I seemed to hear certain speakers deny or devalue certain aspects of human life. I felt fragmented, pulled apart, as though they were saying that parts of me were acceptable while others weren't. Yet I couldn't understand how I could separate the physical from the mental, the emotional from the intellectual, the sexual from the spiritual. I talked to many people. I questioned, raged, and cried.

On Sunday morning, things fell into focus when a loudspeaker boomed through the hall interrupting a speech on evangelism:

Dateline: Pentagon—Sunday, April 16, 1972, B-52's bomb Haiphong. Indochina war escalates.

Dateline: Jerusalem—Isaiah reporting: "Thus says the Lord. I cannot endure iniquity and solemn assemblies. Even though you make prayers I will not listen. Your hands are full of blood."

Dateline: Minneapolis—Two thousand Mennonites gathered in Minneapolis covenant together to pray for peace and to cease paying for war. Correction. Correction. The above has not been confirmed. We will now return to our regular programing.

There was a stunned silence. Tears ran down my cheeks. Swirling in my mind was the image of a Cross, a Man's face contorted with anguish and pain; then an image of bombs, planes, and frightened screaming people. I was engulfed with a clean sadness, not the familiar depression I knew too well. While the speaker prayed, I wept.

We broke into small groups. While the others talked of returning home better evangelists, I wept. The others talked excitedly without acknowledging my tears; I was both grateful and angry. I had gained new insight into myself, into my husband: awareness that all of us are threatened by change, new ideas, and different words. I sensed what seemed a stronger and clearer call to Christ. I was off the hook. I didn't fear damnation and hellfire anymore. I could stop fighting God and the church because—in spite of what some people say and do—it is all right to struggle, to doubt, and to fail. That was an important turning point. From then on, things began to fall into place.

Unlike some who can put up a good front and hide their inner turmoil, my feelings have always flashed across my face like a neon sign, attracting fellow sufferers like bees to honey. Now I made friends. I listened to others. I saw new patterns, new opportunities. I didn't feel isolated anymore. I read five or six books a week: feminist literature, psychology, philosophy, and theology. I listened to Jesus Christ Superstar, weeping with and for the human Christ who died, rejected by an insane uptight world. I shared my poetry. I read the Bible, especially books like Genesis, Samuel, and the Gospels, overwhelmed by the frank portrayal of raw human experience. I participated in a women's group. I went to a writers' conference. I preached a sermon at church.

By that time Earl was also in therapy and had started on his own pilgrimage. He no longer put up with me out of guilt. He had his own needs, needs that conflicted with mine. He joined a men's group. We fought and fought. He disapproved of my activities, my public speaking and going to conferences. Sex was my Achilles' heel; the children were his. He felt inadequate in coping with them. When threatened, he'd retreat behind sarcasm or enforce rigid discipline, devastating the kids. Then I'd find myself trying to shield them from his criticism and wrath.

By now I felt fairly self-confident away from home. I was still reading every chance I got. The women's movement gave me an outlet for my rage. The commission on home ministries asked three of us from the Women's Missionary Association (now called Women in Mission, to reflect our new self-image) to serve on the commission. Working with the commission opened up a new world to me, a world in which I began to experience myself as a man's equal without needing to sacrifice my femininity or becoming hard and businesslike. They allowed me to nurture without making cookies. They gave me new challenges and opportunities and treated me as an equal instead of a threat. They literally loved me back to life.

I was so happy when I was doing things with them that I began to suspect that neither Earl nor I was as neurotic as our therapy had led us to believe; it was our concepts of male-female relationships that were screwed up. Many of my interests, abilities, and talents lay outside of homemaking. Gourmet cooking, crafts, and decorating were interesting but they did not substitute for literature, writing, or theology. I began to see that much of our problem lay in my needing other outlets for my energy since I had more drive than the family could begin to absorb.

I decided to go back to school. My therapist flipped. He was still convinced that my problem stemmed from my resisting my femininity. "When Tim is ten, then you can go," he said. "By then the children will be self-sufficient. They need you at home right now." Wait till Tim is ten! I looked back over the past few years, at the turmoil and hell we'd all been through, and I knew it couldn't go on. For everyone's sake I had to find another outlet for my energy, whether or not it threatened my husband and the American Psychiatric Association.

Reading Phyllis Chesler's book, *Women and Madness,* clinched it. I enrolled in seminary and quit therapy. I was scared silly. I wrote to a friend, "I feel like I'm on the end of a limb that hangs out over a cliff and the rest of the world is back there buzzing away with a chain saw." My mother and Earl's folks couldn't understand why I wanted to go. Earl resented the late meals, a messy house. The girls didn't understand why I needed to study instead of baking cookies or taking them places. Tim thought I should stay at home and play with him. John cried every morning at nursery school. Every symptom of discontent, emotional stress, or frustration I interpreted as my failure.

The transition period was long and painful. I almost quit school several times, but my women's group cheered me on. My struggle was their struggle. They reminded me that going back to school was the most loving thing for everyone in my family—but, oh, I felt guilty. Every time I turned on the radio or television, listened to a sermon or picked up a magazine or newspaper, I seemed to see someone blaming women for the ills of the world.

Earl's and my marital insecurity made each of us desperately jealous of each other. He'd felt inadequate with the kids when I was doing everything. Now that I was in school and involved in other activities, he suddenly found himself giving the boys a bath, running the car pool, and making supper. Unskilled and unsure of himself, he resisted every change with every ounce of his energy.

But I loved school. Now I had a forum in which I could really go to town. I sank my teeth into theology and religious education. Women friends shared my enthusiasm and interests. I was so full that it spilled over and I began talking theology to Earl. He seemed fascinated, which blew my mind.

By that time, I'd thrown aside a lot of religious baggage, and the Bible leapt to life with intense vitality. I reexamined the role of women in the biblical narratives. I noted that they were not passive patsies but activists. I noted that Jesus dealt directly with women, not through their husbands or fathers. I noted that Jesus didn't live and die and rise again to save us from making mistakes. He died to save us from the illusion that we can escape our human fallibility by pretending to be perfect and spiritual. Accepting Christ, then, meant accepting my humanity. Being human meant sharing my brokenness to help others become comfortable with who and what they are. I could do that because Christ's forgiveness and resurrection guaranteed me an open future, no matter what.

Things improved at home. Earl and I were talking to each other. We were more honest in sharing our feelings, more supportive and willing to value each other's views, but I still functioned better away from home. Earl was still threatened by some of my ventures and was especially bewildered by my sexual struggle, which seemed to get worse when I didn't have creative outlets outside the home. I wanted his approval and love so badly that I tried to do almost anything to avoid his criticism and anger.

One evening we got into a heavy argument over my schooling and I ran crying through the orchard behind our house. I shook my fist at the heavens, screaming at God. "How many times will You make me die? You took away Earl's love. You took away my sexual responsiveness. And now You want my school. Do I have to die each time I find something that gives me pleasure and fulfillment?"

In the stillness of that October night, God's answer came. "I will make you die each time that your self-image, dreams, or plans for the future get in the way, when they hurt other people, destroy human relationships, or cut you off from Me. Stop trying to prove to the world that you are a hot-shot. You are My child and that is all that matters. Now go and listen. Be there for others, as I will be there for you."

I didn't go to school the next semester. I worked at rebuilding my relationship with my family. My women's group and several close friends had a way of keeping me honest, as did Earl. They'd cut through my self-pity and defensiveness, forcing me to grow. One evening Earl put his arms around me. "Go back to school. That's where you belong."

I returned to school, and we made a lot of progress in accepting each other and our differences. We took a Parent Effectiveness Training Course together and worked at developing some goals and procedures with the children.

I began to understand I didn't really need Earl in the same way anymore. I'd found my center in Christ. I'd become my own person and no longer saw myself as an extension of my husband.

I asked myself the hard questions I'd managed to avoid for so long. Before, I had needed my husband to validate my reason for being. But if I were to be true to myself and God, then the most loving thing for all of us was to face reality and stop our destructive games. I reread the story of Christ in the garden and wept bitter tears. But I was at peace. I didn't know what lay ahead but that was all right. I was confident that whatever it was, we'd all make it. God was with us. We stopped talking about separating.

A friend once said to me, "I am first of all a child of God, and second a wife and mother." I agree with that sequence. As individuals we can relate in marriage and parenthood only when we have our own center. Jesus' love and forgiveness give us permission to stop pretending and to accept our feelings, behavior, and decisions. All those Christian writers who see women as extensions of men are wrong. As long as I needed my husband as my go-between with God and the world, I fed on him and our children like a parasite. Jesus said that Mary chose the better part—not to negate families, homemaking, or marriage, but to put women's roles in perspective. In God's eyes all his children are equal and are equally responsible for their lives and actions.

In many ways, things haven't changed very much. We still have far to go, much to learn. But life is different. The mood has changed. Most of the tension and guilt are gone. We laugh instead of cry, for we are accepting ourselves and each other. We still disagree over some things, but if we make a mistake, it isn't the end of the world. If something doesn't get done today, there is tomorrow. If I don't make a good grade on an exam, that doesn't mean I haven't learned anything. If I don't respond the way some male sexologist thinks I should, who cares? We just do the best we can because we don't have to prove anything to anybody.

I had run from pain, anger, and failure for so long because I thought they indicated weakness. Now I know differently. The Cross does not call me to be a puppet, an extension of my husband, or an emotionless follower who parrots the right words. The Cross calls me to assume responsibility, to make difficult decisions, to value my own feelings and opinions as well as others', and to move to a Strength beyond myself. It calls me to risk hurt as an enriching part of life and to accept fun and happiness as my right, not a reward for good behavior. Instead of the Cross freeing me from life's burdens, it is the place where I find the courage to face whatever problems I have to face—without neurotic fear. That's why I see my story as a love story, God's love story. His love, his forgiveness, his permission to risk an unknown future, have set me free.

Chapter Thirteen

Virginia Ramey Mollenkott

THE FACE OF SATAN grinned at me from the delivery-room lights as I made my first entry into the world. "You are a damned soul," he articulated carefully, still grinning.

I awoke from that dream several years ago with a vivid memory of that face, and remember it to this day.

I was in high school before I learned that when my parents had discovered I was on my way, there had been talk of an abortion because I was arriving only fourteen months after my brother. I still don't know whether or in what fashion a fetus can "know," or a newborn baby can "remember," what was never conscious. I do know that the theme of damnation has been one of the recurrent motifs of my life. Theologian Mary Daly might explain such a recurrence as the "general feeling of hopelessness, guilt, and anxiety over social disapproval" that results from patriarchal society's casting women in the role of the Female Other who is the cause of all Evil.

Fortunately, however, there has been another recurrent

Virginia Ramey Mollenkott, Ph.D., is professor of English at William Paterson College (New Jersey) and author of four books including Women, Men, and the Bible *(Abingdon, 1977). Active in the Conference on Christianity and Literature, the Milton Society of America, and the Modern Language Association, she has published many articles in religious, educational, and literary journals.*

theme in my life. When I was about ten years old, sitting alone in my grandmother's sunny breakfast room, I selected as my "life verse" the passage in which the apostle Paul summarized his career: "I do not consider myself yet to have taken hold of it. But one thing I do: Forgetting what is behind and straining toward what is ahead, I press on toward the goal to win the prize for which God has called me heavenward in Christ Jesus" (Phil. 3:13–14, NIV).

At that time I had no awareness of *process* versus *stasis,* of *becoming* as opposed to *being*—at least not by name. Yet I freely identified with the apostle's sense of process—even though nothing in my environment as a young girl ever encouraged me to think that I could someday be a worker in the theological arena. The closest I could approach such a role was to yearn to become a missionary. If I sensed that on the mission field a woman would be allowed a fuller role in the life of the church (because most men were uninterested in being missionaries), the realization was unconscious. Yet sitting here at my typewriter at age forty-four, in the midst of a career as an English professor and amateur theologian, I can recognize in myself exactly the same urges that led me over three decades ago to choose those Bible verses as my motto. Now, however, I understand more of what it means to forget what is behind and strain toward what is ahead. I have also begun to learn the importance of selective remembering and of less straining.

I was brought up in Philadelphia in the Plymouth Brethren assemblies, where men spoke as they were moved by the Holy Spirit but women knew that the Holy Spirit would never lead them to be anything but silent. Nevertheless, I preached to my playmates, sometimes gathering them on the front steps of our row house in order to hold forth about their need for salvation.

When my father left home forever, I was nine years old. I was not permitted to see him at all, and sometimes I lay on his bed crying for him. By the time I was in high school I was sneaking to see him, meeting him in subways or parks. There was an aura of the forbidden, an aura of glamor, around him. When my mother found out that I was seeing him, without delay she sent me away to a private Christian school.

There the administration provided plentiful reinforcement

for my feeling of damnation. After only a few weeks, I was called to the office under a terrible but mysterious cloud. There were dire looks; did I understand the horror of what I had done? Trembling and without the slightest idea of what they were talking about, I admitted that yes, I knew. Would I be willing to undergo any punishment they decided upon, or would I prefer to be sent home in disgrace? Fearing my mother's wrath, I said I would take any punishment they decided upon. The punishment for my unknown crime turned out to be that, although my mother was paying full tuition rates, I would have to work as if I were on a tuition scholarship. Thus I entered the world of the slave-laborer, working with the "missionary kids" at the most menial jobs instead of having the privileges of the "fully paid."

It was only when I went home for Christmas and was met by a thin-lipped unsmiling mother that I found out what my crime had been: I had "forcibly stripped" a girl! The head of the school had written that wild story to my mother, who had believed it without so much as asking me whether I was guilty.

I pointed out to my mother that even if I were a violent person with a passionate desire to "strip" other girls, there would have been no reason to do so in the hideously immodest surroundings of dorm life. Two unpartitioned toilets and two bathtubs stood in the middle of their respective bathrooms, to be shared by twenty girls, many of whom ran around naked morning, noon, and night. I had been overwhelmed with embarrassment at the setup and sought through all sorts of subterfuge to find a time when I could use those facilities in private. When I had explained all this, my mother seemed sorry she had so readily sided against me. We searched high and low for the incriminating letter, intending to threaten a lawsuit; but no letter could be found. To me it did not seem terribly strange that my mother had sided against me. It was all part of being a damned soul.

Back I went to that school, where I was seriously overworked but determined to prove myself a good child of God. Occasionally, one of the staff members would take pains to tell me that there was no room in God's service for people like me. For some reason, I never could bring myself to defend myself or tell them that their accusation had been totally false. Despite

their discouragements, I memorized Scripture doggedly, trying
to fill my mind night and day with the Word of the Lord and
crying out to him whenever I was told that I was useless in
his sight. The fact that I never gave up seems to suggest that
deep inside I was more convinced that I was "pressing toward
the goal" than I was of my own damnation. I clung to the
promises of Scripture and tried to convince myself that I didn't
need any human comfort as long as I had the Lord.

But since the school administration refused to let me have
any special friends of either sex and policed my activities carefully, I was excruciatingly lonely. The only spiritual encouragement from adults during my three years there came from a
missionary from Dohnavour, the home base of the great missionary Amy Carmichael. Although the school claimed to have
modeled itself on Carmichael's principles, that Dohnavour missionary felt very uncomfortable in its elitist atmosphere. She
later told my aunt that I was one of the few genuine Christians
she had met there. When I heard that unusual estimate of
myself, I wept with relief.

I spent my college years at Bob Jones University trying to
sort out my personal vocation and desperately striving for spiritual perfection. During my senior year I dated a man who
seemed to me the strong, silent type. Not having grown up
around any male other than my artistic and articulate brother,
whose chief delight lay in tormenting me, I thought that I
preferred strong, silent types. The dating rules at Bob Jones
were perfectly calculated to keep men and women from getting to know each other well: a few hours a week in the dating
parlor, sitting at least six inches apart under the watchful eyes
of chaperones; going to vespers together once a week; walking
home from meals and meetings at that respectable six inches
or more. No touching, no hugging, no kissing. Under such external restraints, many of us became obsessed. It was easy to misin-
terpret the thrill of the "forbidden" as feelings of genuine love.
Something told me that I should not marry that person, that
we weren't right for each other, but the advice I was given
by various teachers was that love comes after marriage, and
not to worry about that.

Within hours of the wedding ceremony, I was convinced
that I had made a terrific mistake but equally convinced that

I would have to live with it for the rest of my life. Because of her own painful experiences, Mother had often said that men could not be trusted; I was probably proving her point by marrying someone completely unsuitable to my personality. Of course I wasn't consciously aware of that. But I *was* dimly aware of the fact that marriage was the only route by which I could claim adulthood and remove myself from family domination. What I didn't know at all was how many of my human rights I was surrendering in the eyes of the law and in the eyes of the church.

I had seventeen years during which to learn those lessons. I worked part time the first year of marriage, full time all the other years, in addition to earning an M.A. and a Ph.D. But although he was not supporting me and barely supporting himself, my husband saw no reason why he should not relax when he came in from work while I returned from work to prepare our dinner. Afterward, he watched TV while I washed our dishes, cleaned our house, washed and ironed our clothes, and then studied or graded papers until after midnight.

I'm not sure that even I realized how wrong that arrangement was. I wasn't getting so much as food and lodging in return for my labors. My husband dropped his socks wherever he happened to be sitting when he took them off; it was my job to pick them up, since I was a woman. If I complained, I felt guilty for being a nag. I knew that our marriage wasn't fair by human standards, but we were Christians and were supposed to live by biblical standards. The Bible said that women were to submit to their husbands. I couldn't think too much about it for fear of madness.

After about five years, I made the classic mistake of thinking that a child would somehow save our marriage. And indeed, I loved everything about being pregnant except for the dehumanizing treatment from my male gynecologist and the hospital staff. I never had morning sickness. I taught my college classes until graduation and had the baby in early July.

I was overjoyed to have a son. I had prayed for a son and had continued to hope for one even when the doctor had predicted a girl. At the time I thought I wanted a son because I felt girls were too complex for me to cope with. Now I recognize that I wanted to bring into the world a first-class citizen,

not a second-class one, though I couldn't have admitted that
to myself at the time. If hard personal study of the Bible had
forced me to admit firsthand that God's Word insists on the
necessary subjugation of half of the human race, my sense of
justice would have caused such devastating conflict that I might
have been forced to abandon my faith. Without the goal in
Christ Jesus to strive toward, who would I be? I couldn't let
myself think about it.

While my son was still a baby I decided I'd better begin
on a Ph.D. I had been teaching English for years and knew
exactly what I wanted from a doctoral program. I enrolled at
New York University, and despite sole responsibility for our
child and the household chores and family finances and the
English department which I chaired, I finished my degree in
six years. The Superwoman act. In the process I broke my
health.

I remember lying alone in the guest bedroom for days, growing dehydrated because my son was too small and my husband
too unconcerned to bring me adequate liquids. I felt that I
was dying.

About that time I began hearing regularly from a student
I had taught years before, a single woman ten years my junior
who lived in Tacoma, Washington. She was by that time a
public school teacher, and she mentioned that she would like
to visit me that following summer. During her visit she saw
what was happening to me; and to my amazement she decided
to get a job in the east and lift much of the housework from
my shoulders. A year later, she did exactly that.

Even with Lynne's physical help and spiritual supportiveness, my recovery was slow: it took years of a high-powered
nutritional program, increased rest, and a succession of doctors.
In the long run, chiropractic and vitamins did more for me
than all the M.D.'s and their drugs. As I began to grow stronger
and began to believe that I would live and not die, I also began
to think about the possibility of ending my long marital
servitude.

During my doctoral program I had become a Milton special-
ist, and of course had read Milton's four treatises on divorce.
I was aware that although the Plymouth Brethren considered
divorce a dreadful sin, Milton was a godly man who read the

New Testament differently. He pointed out that nowhere in the New Testament is the body treated as more important than the soul; why, then, should "adultery" be interpreted only as a physical act, when spiritual adultery—including the lack of supportiveness and compatibility—was so much harder to bear? What God had joined together, certainly no person should put asunder. But when two people had blundered into a yoke which caused both or one of them misery because they were unsuited to each other, it was obvious that *God* had not joined them together.

Although I was by no means convinced of the accuracy of Milton's line of thought, it was nevertheless germinating in my mind. Still, the thought of leaving my husband filled me with dread. I feared the reactions of my family; I feared the effect on my career as a Christian author; and above all, I did not want to deprive my son of his father as I had been deprived of mine.

Ultimately, my decision was made easier by my son. He began to sleep only with great difficulty, and frequently he drew pictures of faraway houses. I took him to a psychologist, who eventually told me that his condition would not improve until I made up my mind firmly about my future. Children could tell when their parents were trying to hold a marriage together for the sake of the children, the psychologist explained, and Paul was suffering from a sense of guilt at thinking he was the cause of my unhappiness. "Better come from a broken home than live in one," the psychologist said. And besides, he questioned, hadn't I suffered enough?

Yes. I had suffered enough. Within a month I moved out, taking our child and the cat and my own possessions and dividing with my husband everything that had been purchased jointly. At first we lived in the temporarily empty house of an old friend. Because rents in the area were unreasonably high, I wanted to buy a home. I discovered that because of dower rights, no real-estate company would give me a mortgage until the divorce was finalized. I knew that that would be a long time coming, since my husband was threatening to contest it. Ultimately, I pooled my resources with Lynne and together we bought a lakeside house in her name. Only after the divorce were we able to switch to joint ownership.

Things were tight financially because much of my money was tied up in the house I had bought with my husband, and he had vowed that I would never get back a penny of that. It was like starting all over again. But I never doubted that I had done what had to be done. I felt enormously relieved, my son began to brighten up, and best of all, his father began to be a real father to him. Before the separation, he had been full of harsh words for his son, apparently viewing such abuse as a way of hurting me. But the shock of discovering that the marriage was really ended seemed to change all that. I assumed complete financial and personal responsibility for the boy but made no restrictions on the number of phone calls and visits to his father. They soon were numerous, and continue to be.

Between the time of my separation and that of my divorce, I began to read secular feminist literature, largely because of a friend I met on a Christian tour to Italy at which I had been a token woman speaker. My new friend was an ardent feminist; and although she wondered why the Bible should matter so much to me, she tolerated my timid first attempts to understand the Bible's message for women because she could also see the growth of my involvement in the secular movement. About that time I was very much encouraged to see feminist articles concerning the Bible in *Christianity Today:* one by Ruth Schmidt (see Appendix 2), the other by Letha Scanzoni. Shortly thereafter I was invited to present an overview of the "women's movement" at a theological conference on women. It was at that conference that I met Paul Jewett, Letha Scanzoni, and Nancy Hardesty.

During the conference, Paul Jewett gave me a new lease on life by taking seriously my exegetical abilities and by saying I had spoken like a prophet. Only someone who has endured years of put-downs and the ignoring or mockery of her gifts could possibly appreciate the impact of such male approval. In contrast, my former husband had frequently warned me that he could tell God not to listen to my prayers, and God would cut me off. (To my knowledge, he still believes that husbands have that kind of ultimate spiritual predominance over their wives.)

Once the theological conference had ended, Letha Scanzoni began to write me long encouraging letters. The publication of the Scanzoni-Hardesty book, *All We're Meant to Be,* was of course the real impetus for the whole "evangelical feminist" movement. With Letha's constant support, I spent five years studying the Bible's message about male-female relationships in home and church. I delivered a summary of my findings as the keynote speech of the first national conference of the Evangelical Women's Caucus, and a few weeks later Abingdon Press asked me to write a book and prepare a cassette lecture series on the topic of *Women, Men, and the Bible.*

Frequently I have heard people blame feminism for the increasing divorce rates in America. I have been very hesitant to let people know about my divorce for fear they would assume that the divorce discredits any message that God has given me to speak or write. But the fact is that feminism had nothing to do with my divorce; the proceedings were well underway before I ever thought of myself as a feminist. What feminism did do was help to heal my relationships with myself and with others and with God. Evangelical feminism with its national network of supportive love has confirmed in me the conviction that I am not a damned soul but rather a woman of God in process, pressing toward that goal in Christ Jesus.

Christians are now beginning to study the Word of God more deeply concerning divorce. More and more godly people are learning that like everything else, divorce is not beyond the reach of God's forgiving and restoring love. Those who are willing to be honest about the facts are openly recognizing that the American patriarchal family got into trouble with the rise of industrialism, whereas the current women's movement did not gain momentum until the mid-sixties. The marriages currently breaking were not formed under the influence of feminism, but rather under the influence of traditional attitudes and sex-role stereotypes. More and more Christians are coming to realize that egalitarian principles are completely consonant with biblical teaching about the mutual submission of each Christian to every other Christian. Evangelical feminism is thus offering to people the principles that may well be the saving of the family.

According to my observations and studies, it is true that some marriages have been broken after one member found fulfillment and authenticity through the outside support of men's or women's consciousness-raising groups. But it is also true that many marriages have been strengthened when both members recognized the good news of equal partnership in Christ and were willing to make the effort to grow simultaneously. If a marriage is based on mutual authentic caring, the heightening of awareness and a new sense of human equality will not undermine it.

As for my life today, I have never felt as challenged, as joyful, as fulfilled. I am successfully completing a four-year term as chairwoman of a large state college English department. I am surrounded by supportive friends and beckoning opportunities. There are many failures, many struggles; as T. S. Eliot puts it, "We are undefeated only because we have gone on trying." But on the wall next to my desk, beside my print of Rembrandt's head of Christ, is a message someone sent to me after the Washington conference of the Evangelical Women's Caucus: "To Virginia, a chosen one of God, a prophet and sister. To remember Washington, 1975, and with a sense of awe that you shared yourself with strangers. Shalom." How can one feel like a damned soul, surrounded by such love? Christ's love shown through human persons encourages me toward confidence that I am not damned, but chosen. Shalom, indeed. The peace that passes understanding. All the way to the goal.

Chapter Fourteen

Lois C. Andersen

DOCTOR, I FEEL *so irritable and depressed! Do you think it might be the Pill?*

How often I have to assess that question. It's my job. For over twenty years I have worked with women. First with the mothers of young children, in the field of pediatrics. Then in suburbia as a full-time housewife myself, mother of five, and wife of a clergyman. Then back into medicine, working solely with women. All the time listening, listening, listening.

Doctor, I just can't keep going. I'm frazzled. There's too much to do, and I'm never finished.

In three countries—Australia, America, New Zealand—I have lived and watched and listened. I have searched and struggled in my own mind, trying to find out what God wants of me as a twentieth-century woman. Until I find my own way to wisdom, how can I help my sister? Should I try? Am I my sister's keeper? It is the plight of my fellow-strugglers, women I love and ache for, that gives impetus to my attempts to think through the problems that come to so many women today.

Doctor, I'm so rebellious, I feel guilty, confused. I love my

---

Lois C. Andersen, MB. BS. (M.D.), lives in Sydney, Australia, and has a general practice with special interest in women. She and her husband Francis are the parents of five children.

*husband, my two little boys. But we can't go on this way. I
have weeping fits. Then I find myself resenting my family. I
have such a yearning to get back to teaching. I had a couple
of years of it before I got married, and I loved it. Now I'm
"only a housewife." I feel a nothing—not even a good
mother . . .*

*Doctor, I'm always tired. Yes, I'm working full time—we're
saving up to buy a house. No, I don't spend any money on
household help. No, my husband doesn't help me much with
"women's work." He expects me to manage the way his mother
did, and I know she did have outside help. And then he has
his meetings. I guess I'm resentful inside most of the time because I have two full-time jobs. I'm sharing the bread-winning;
but he doesn't share the homemaking . . .*

*Lois, I feel rebellious, frustrated, guilty. I've been married
only a year, and I've come up against this whole question of
"submission." I used to be an Inter-Varsity staffworker, and
suddenly my world shrank. I feel so restive. Dick wants me
to be at home full time. He says he can provide for both of
us, and he likes to think of me there. A family hasn't happened
to us yet, and being at home isn't enough for me. I want to
seize the opportunity to go on toward an M.A., but Dick says
he's the head of the family, and he expects me to be submissive.
I know the Bible says that wives should submit, but . . .*

It would be easy to fall into the medical trap of quickly pre-
scribing a tranquilizer—or accepting the frequent reality that
hormonal side-effects of the Pill sometimes cause depression.
But my own experience as a housewife and as a mother has
increased my sensitivity to basic human problems. Gentle prob-
ing often uncovers resentments and deep conflicts.

As I think about these things, I realize that although the
plight of others first stimulated my conscious search for answers, many incidents in my own life had already triggered
in me confusion, heartache, frustration. It was not in the marriage relationship that I had my problems. I had married in
the spirit of Ephesians 5, being determined that unless I met
a man whom I could admire, whose judgment I could trust,
and who I felt loved me with something of the spirit of that
chapter, I would rather not marry at all. That was how I had
prayed for years. I had seen too many mediocre marriages,

Christian and otherwise. I wanted none of them. After all, I had a career that was completely fascinating.

I married when I was twenty-nine, and Christian marriage as my husband and I found and forged it has been far beyond anything I had visualized: partnership, comradeship of minds, radiance, and love. Much of that harmony, though, was developed in the ups and downs of adjustment and growth—so that I now wonder, "Has our marriage succeeded because it was grounded in the spirit of Ephesians 5—with those unpalatable notions of submission and headship? Or, more likely, was it that we instinctively realized that we were not a first-century couple, and unconsciously and creatively adapted that early Christian model to a living twentieth-century relationship?"

In mutual respect and mutual submission we had lost nothing of enduring Christian principles. Certainly as I look back over our many years of marriage, "submission" hasn't seemed to be a conscious part of the scene. It was rather each caring first for the other's happiness.

The biblical teaching that the man is the "head" of the woman is still a challenge to us as we try to transpose its truth into a twentieth-century setting. In the feelings of many Christian women, and in the assertions of many Christian men, headship implies a superior-inferior relationship. In many marriages, authority is abused by the male and endured by the female in a way that would not be tolerated anywhere else in a democratic society. Theologically, such an emphasis on headship is confusing—for the clear, overall picture we find in the New Testament is that in Christ no one is intrinsically superior to anyone else. The greatest person is the one who makes himself or herself the "least" (see Mark 10:35-45 and many other passages). So what do we do with "headship"? If not intrinsic, is it functional?

In practice, with a large and lively family to handle, it has been a relief to me (when appropriate) to resort to my husband's position of authority as the leader of our family unit. But his expression of that authority has not been even remotely suppressing. Rather he has sought ways to release each member to develop his or her own potential—and especially me, his wife. I realize I have been blessed. I have seen Christian marriages where a "very biblical" husband wields his authority with a heavy hand, quoting the usual texts in order to keep his wife "in her place."

In the changing phases of our marriage we have shared both the bread-winning and the homemaking, so that each could be free to develop careers and interests as the situation demanded. But with me the family came first, my career second. That was my choice, my interpretation of my calling as a mother. As the requirements of family life changed, I had to accept the challenge to adapt my style of life in order to integrate two jobs—home and work; or, when not working professionally, home and my other outside interests. Sometimes it has seemed difficult. But it has been a rich, full, and varied adventure.

It was trying to find my role as a woman in society, and particularly as a woman in the church, that caused my main personal struggle. I had studied medicine at the University of Melbourne (Australia). I had come from a particularly conservative and restrictive church background, where women were given incredibly minimal opportunity for ministry of any kind. University life was therefore a liberating and exhilarating experience. In my training years I gradually became accustomed to being treated as a human person, equal with my male colleagues. The women, though few in proportion, did well academically. A woman topped our class my graduating year. Afterward, in the early years of my career, there was little or no sexual discrimination on the hospital scene. If a woman was competent, she was respected. The men did not appear to find it a problem to accept the guidance and authority of a medical colleague of senior rank or experience, if the superior person happened to be female. I flourished happily in that environment. I was accepted in group discussions, medical or otherwise, as an equal, as a person with a mind. I began to take it for granted.

It came as a shock, therefore, when we left Australia in 1963 because of my husband's work, and settled in California. Abruptly I was transported from a man's world to a woman's world, and it was hard to take. Geography wasn't the cause. In fact, generally speaking, women have more scope in America than in Australia. But in my case the contrast was made more dramatic by the fact that I was not permitted to practice medicine. On a previous visit I had been a fellow in pediatrics as an exchange visitor in the Johns Hopkins Hospital in Baltimore. But to secure a license as a permanent resident of California, I was required not only to sit for many examinations (fair enough; we require the same of immigrants in our own country), but also to do two years' full-time internship.

By that time I had had over ten years' experience in the field of pediatrics—and had four children of my own. In Australia I had developed a very satisfactory pattern of working two days a week, thus earning enough to have adequate household help. So I was still able to give plenty of time to my husband and children. To contemplate now spending two years in full-time hospital work—including weekends and often nights—when I had four young children to mother, seemed to me irresponsible. In spite of much inquiry, there was no other way. It seemed that I had to forfeit medicine.

Regulations and working conditions of that kind are common in professional spheres. Such requirements are made by men, and they "work" for men. They are quite unrealistic for a woman who is a wife and mother.

I missed those two days per week in the world of medicine more than I had dreamed possible. I missed just as much the acceptance of myself as an equal person in society. I was no longer accepted as such. I was "only a housewife." How often I have heard women say that: internalizing in their self-image the estimation that society gives them. It was sometimes amusing to notice how people's attitude toward me would change if they found out that I wasn't "just a housewife"; I was a doctor. I came to see how phony and unchristian it was to esteem any person, male or female, for professional achievements and status.

Of many incidents I could narrate, I recall one when we were on sabbatical leave. My husband had accepted an invitation to spend three months in a missionary situation. He had plenty to do in lectures and workshops. I found myself in a new society. What would my "place" be? Often I felt like a shadow or a hole in the air. My husband was listened to, appreciated, respected. I was his wife; that was my only identity, my only significance. I found it very depressing. It had nothing to do with jealousy or a desire for the limelight. I loved my husband and rejoiced more than anyone in his achievements. After all, we were part of each other. We were "one flesh" in the eyes of God and in our own eyes. But others did not seem to share that view.

I think that if I went back to such a situation now, I have learned enough of life, of God, of myself, to cope and to learn. But when I was a young mother, that episode raised questions that I had to grapple with at greater depth.

We spent ten years in California. For ten years I lived in only half my world. During that time of translation into a completely woman's world, I had to grapple with spending all my time doing housework. As an absolutely full-time occupation— I mean full-time, not just thirty-five hours a week like most workers—it gradually became depressing. Why should that be? There was nothing wrong with our family. We had every happiness. Yet the reasons for housewife blues are obvious. The problem is universal for the modern woman, especially if she has some education. So much of housework is repetitive, boring, frustrating, never-ending, and with limited scope for creativity. There is so little to show for all that effort. There is no recognition or appreciation in society at large. A housewife is outshone in glamor by what "interesting" people do. I was always tired, never finished, constantly feeling inadequate.

Who ever feels adequate as a young parent—especially in these times when the nurture of a family is so difficult, so frequently ending in breakdown and delinquency? Mistakes are noticed—but not successes. And all the time, there is work, work, work. In a servantless age the sheer volume of physical work required by a large family is somehow destroying.

I found housework more exhausting than being on duty for ninety hours a week as an intern in a hospital. Add to that the loneliness with very small children and no adult company all day. The sense of being intellectually starved could bring on panic: Is the whole of my life to be like this?

Women's liberation spokespersons were saying: "Just take the children along to the child-care center, and be released 'from all that.' Develop your own identity in the real world. Do your own thing." Did I agree with that line of thought? No. My years in pediatrics had alerted me to a danger. Love is not to be bought. You cannot pay someone to love your

child. Housewives are justly outraged because of the mean
value that society puts on them. But their true dignity cannot
be gained by communicating to their children that they are
a nuisance and an encumbrance, to be disposed of so that their
mothers can do more important things than child-raising.

There is a vast difference between a mother's working part
time and working full time outside the home, especially during
the vital years of infancy and early childhood—the worst years
for many mothers. Part-time child care need not jeopardize
the parent-child relationship; full-time child care is fraught with
risks. The risks have to be weighed. Much depends on the
urgency of the situation, and much depends on the genuine
love of the substitute mother.

I was fortunate in this matter. When forced to work full
time because of family needs, I was able to have my mother
or my sister as substitute parent. Their help actually enriched
my children's involvement in our extended family. Yet I would
never advise full-time work for a mother of small children,
except for a limited time, and only if there were no other
solution.

As I struggled to come to terms with this problem for my
own peace of mind, I had to wrestle—not in theory, but in
reality—with what it means to be a woman, what it means
to be a wife, a mother, to respond again to a fresh sense of
mission as a twentieth-century Christian. I gradually learned
that much can be done to meet the needs of the full-time
housewife. Once you identify those needs, you can do something about the loneliness, the terrific fatigue. There is plenty
that can be done to keep up intellectual interests. There is
always a ministry, if you long to reach out to other hurting
and lonely people.

Yet the most difficult part of all was the feeling that I was
a second-class citizen. I found it difficult to accept the apparent
insignificance of my life in society, and in the church, when
compared with that of a man. Gradually my self-esteen was
chipped away. It had been hammered into me by implication
and attitude year after year in the church that my husband
and his work were of much more significance than me and
my work. Was that true? I had to search out afresh my value
in the eyes of God. Coming to terms with it was hard, but

brought great release. Wasn't my response to God a commitment to mission as much as anybody's? I had been willing to
go off and serve God as a missionary doctor; now I had been
called to wash dishes in California.

The brief painful experience I mentioned during Frank's
sabbatical was therapeutic. My role-uncertainty there forced
me to face the problem of my self-worth, and work it out honestly with God. It was not something to be suppressed, ignored,
or smothered with pious words that I shouldn't feel that way
if I was "really spiritual." I had seen enough shriveled and
stunted human lives to know psychologically that the human
person needs to feel accepted and appreciated in order to
thrive. I was nourished marvelously in this way by my husband.
But I needed to be reassured that being a woman didn't dimin-
ish my acceptance and value to my Lord.

Gradually I found that assurance in the Scripture. The apostle
Paul saw clearly the dignity and importance of all members
of Christ's body, however diverse their functions, however
lowly their station. Since resolving this matter, the question
of whether the church considers my contribution of any significance is immeasurably less important to me. To have peace
with God as an equally loved and valued child of his, no matter
what attitudes I meet constantly in the church—that is the
sheet-anchor I had to gain by passing through the fires of those
experiences.

It was the late sixties. Women's groups had emerged all over
America. All kinds of questions were being asked. Bibles had
been burned in the streets of Berkeley by militants, protesting
against a Puritan heritage with its suppression of women. Many
young women whom I knew at that time were confused and
troubled. And the ones most torn apart were those who ac-
knowledged the supreme importance and authority of the
teachings of the Bible in every part of their lives; the ones
honest enough to see discrepancies and difficulties in the Bible's
estimation of women. There was much that didn't make sense.
Many of them opened their hearts to me.

For eighteen months three of us (the other two were young
Inter-Varsity staff workers) researched the question: What do

we, as twentieth-century women who believe the Bible, do about the women's liberation movement? In our investigations we had to balance our reading of feminist literature, psychology, theology, and historical background with meticulous study of huge chunks of biblical material. I revived my neglected Greek in order to get as close as possible to the text. In fact, by that time I had begun study for a degree in theology, so I was able to integrate the two experiences to some extent.

One night I had just finished a few weeks of reading straight through the Gospels. Then the epistles. The contrast in the attitude toward women of Jesus and Paul hit me hard. Identifying with the situations as a woman, I had felt acceptance as a person by Jesus. With Paul—well, I felt battered, patronized. I wept. I realized that in the past I had closed my eyes to hard sayings that were now staring me in the face.

"Women should remain silent in the churches." "It is a shameful thing for a woman to speak in church." "Man is the image and glory of God; woman is the glory of man. The man is the head of the woman." "I permit no woman to teach, nor to have authority over men."

After those eighteen months, when our mini-workshop had to end as we scattered to different parts of the world, the search didn't end. My husband was a willing resource. My Greek was that of a student, but he is an expert in the original biblical languages. He has a vast knowledge of biblical literature and background. It was, I think, invaluable to have "masculine" as well as "feminine" thinking involved in a project of this kind. Now, after almost ten years of honest reading, prayer, consultation, and pondering, I can read Paul's epistles with appreciation and without heartache.

I have realized that we continually read those letters (indeed, the whole Bible) with twentieth-century ideas in our minds, forgetting the patterns of society in ancient times and the context in which the Bible was written. Hence the tricky question: how do we distinguish the local and cultural elements from the deeper, enduring theological principles? When it comes to the place of women in the Christian community, a number of factors have to be taken into account:

1. The very limited educational opportunities for women in New Testament times made it unlikely that any but the

exceptionally gifted or privileged would be equipped for responsibility in the church, particularly in the area of teaching.

2. Restrictive social customs then prevailing would make it inappropriate, if not offensive, in most communities.

3. Most of the biblical teaching about relationships between men and women lies in the context of marriage. Confusion arises in our day when the teaching is applied in a general way to other relationships.

4. The pattern of marriage at that time, especially in Judaism, and continuing into early Christianity, was suppressive of women. That suppression was the result of a theological distortion, the historical causes of which can be traced.

In view of such factors, I began to realize how revolutionary was the scope of ministry the early church actually accorded to women (see Acts 12:12; 16:14,15,40; 21:9; Rom. 16; 1 Cor. 11:2–16; 16:19; Phil. 4:3; Col. 4:15). It even astonished me that Paul, for his time, in so many instances showed a radical theological awareness of the equality before God of men and women (Gal. 3:26–28). Repeatedly his thrust was not to tear down the limiting social patterns and institutions of that day, but to show how relationships within those frameworks could be transformed "in the Lord." Thus he spoke of the relationship between Jew and Gentile, master and slave, male and female. The epistle to Philemon showed how the master-slave relationship could be transformed by the love of God. Ephesians 5 pointed out how Christian love could transform the restrictive current model of marriage into a beautiful relationship. Concrete social patterns among Christians began changing their outward forms through the sustained impact of that new thinking. The Jew-Gentile dichotomy was already being superseded in the church in New Testament times, and what confusion and resistance there was among the Christians—even the apostle Peter!

It took centuries for the legal framework of slavery to be torn down (although that is not completely accomplished in all countries even yet). Much credit for that emancipation goes to the teaching of Jesus (and Paul), to the initiative of Christians, to the leavening effect of Christian ethics on whole societies. (Even so, there were still Christians who were prepared to quote Scripture in favor of slavery.)

Only in our century has the similar need to overcome prejudice against women and to abolish the restrictions placed on them by society, in custom as well as law, come to sharp consciousness. And confusion and resistance by many Christians is again in evidence. That is understandable—Christian reaction often finds its justification in the extremes to which some militants have gone.

Whatever the cultural framework in any historical period, the challenge to those who are disciples of Christ is to transform all their relationships "in the Lord" (Eph. 6:1—parent-child; Col. 3:18—husband-wife; Phil. 17—master-slave). This suggests that our task as twentieth-century Christians is not to fit ourselves into first-century social patterns, but to live in our contemporary society—Africa, Australia, America, Asia, wherever—scrutinizing it closely, discerning its values, and asking honestly (in any particular matter) if we as Christians should (1) stand against society; (2) follow its normal behavior patterns as part of that society; or (3) accept society's patterns as far as conscience will go, attempting to transform our inner life by Christian love, while trying to change outward social expressions to something nearer the Christian ideal.

I am convinced that the place to begin is within one's own self. We must find peace in our relationship with God as a woman as well as a person. Without that, we will be irritated, frustrated, and belligerent in the church, rather than joyful, patient, and vigorously honest. To be convinced in one's own mind is vital, though there will be ongoing adjustment and growth in this age of transition.

That should be an exciting adventure, and not the wrangling, loveless debate we find in some Christian magazines and churches. Jesus has the last word: "By this everyone will recognize that you are My disciples, if you love one another" (John 13:35 MLB).

Appendix 1

Woman's Work

(from *HIS* magazine, 1960)

"I WAS EXTREMELY pleased to read that you are ending your paid working days. I believe married Christian women belong at home."

This is an excerpt from a letter written by a male friend when he heard that my husband and I had decided that I should be a "full-time" housewife. Implicit in what he wrote, though tactfully omitted, is the idea that the two years I spent after our marriage working as a teacher-librarian were displeasing to God. This attitude I believe is rather common among conservative Christians.

The question in my mind is, "Does God call Christian women to be exclusively housewives?"

It is usually obvious to Christians that most single women ought to have a job. If God wanted a Christian woman to be a homemaker, He would have provided her with a husband. Too few Christians praise God for the single woman who is willing to stay single for His glory. They usually think of marriage as God's unequivocal best (just as most non-Christians do), and Satan has been quick to use this subtle pressure to bring about marriages out of God's will—or at least to rob the single woman of the peace and joy of serving God in her present state.

So the question is amended to, "Does God call married Christian women to be exclusively housewives?" It seems to me that to find the answer a Christian wife must seek to know God's will by (1) examining the teaching of Scripture; (2) examining her own attitudes and motivation prayerfully; and (3) obeying her husband.

What does the Scripture teach about a wife's "place"? Such a question is hard to answer for two reasons. First, the social and cultural mores of Biblical times were quite different from those of mid-twentieth-century America, making it necessary for us to seek the spirit rather than the letter of the law; and second, our minds tend to look for verses to substantiate our own position rather than be taught by the Spirit.

Genesis 2:18 tells why God made woman. "It is not good that the man should be alone; I will make him a helper fit for him." When God made woman as man's helper, He commanded them (not him alone) to subdue the earth. The picture in Eden's perfection seems to be of Adam tending the Garden with his wife's help, of both working, and working together.

The Scripture here pictures a principle that modern marriage counselors emphasize. The jobs of both husband and wife should not be carried on in lonely isolation but should be shared. A wife can often correct papers, send out statements, type letters. A husband can wax floors, carry out garbage, give the baby his bath. A deliberate sharing of jobs (even though some efficiency of operation may be lost) lays a foundation for two important aspects of Christian married life: (1) the opportunity to serve each other as the Lord served those He loved, "bearing one another's burden"; (2) vitality in shared prayer arising out of a shared struggle.*

Paul said, "And I ask you also, true yokefellow, help these women, for they have labored side by side with me in the gospel together with Clement and the rest of my fellow workers, whose names are in the book of life" (Philippians 4:3). Here is another picture of men and women co-working for God.

---

*At this point, the article as originally published, though not as originally written, contained the following interpolation by a male editor:

Of course, the Bible also says that "everyone shall bear his own burden," and couples must be careful lest so much time and thought are spent "helping" the other partner that the work for which each has primary responsibility suffers.

The Scripture which deals most specifically with a good wife's work is Proverbs 31:10–31. She works with willing hands; she brings food from afar; she directs the work of the women under her; she goes to bed late and gets up early; she buys a field and plants a vineyard, she spins thread, weaves cloth and makes clothes; she sells what she has made. Is it overstating the case to conclude that such a wife suggests a modern executive? The wife is literally a "bread-winner." Her husband (who finds his wife "more precious than jewels") would be puzzled with any thought that a wife's activities should be limited to the home.

Of course, it is essential for a Christian wife to find the course in which the Spirit gives her peace. Certainly the heart of the matter lies in having children. The greatest service that many, perhaps most, Christian couples can perform for God is to raise children who love the Lord Jesus. Any work should be subordinated to this. The wife may like or not like her job; the important thing is to seek God's will in the matter rather than her personal preference or a friendly opinion. There is only one Lydia, "seller of purple," in the New Testament; but there is one.

A difficult problem in this area sometimes arises on foreign mission fields. A number of Biblical, evangelical boards appoint both mother and father as "missionaries." The children may therefore be sent away to school or left with servants while the wife works. This hardly seems consistent with the frowns cast by many Biblical Christians on the working woman at home. Perhaps it is the more surprising in view of the problems, moral and otherwise, which confront children in many missionary areas, which would seem to make the mother's influence on her children the more necessary.

In a society saturated with the partnership concept of marriage it seems necessary to point a Christian wife to a third consideration: the wife is to obey her husband. It surprises me to hear of Christian women who have had the word "obey" deleted from their marriage vows. It may be a painful, powerful blow to the intellectual pride of a Christian woman to acknowledge that, like Eve, she is more easily deceived than her husband. It's hard for some Christian women to let their husbands decide a matter about which there is a difference of opinion.

Yet this is all parenthetical to the point that if my husband wants me to work, I should work; if he wants me to stop, I should stop. One woman (a Christian) remarked that it seemed to her that a wife was a slave of her husband. That may be, but if both husband and wife are slaves of Jesus Christ, the relationship is cast in a different light. (Read I Peter 3:1-7; Ephesians 5:21-23.)

Happy then is the Christian wife who finds the place where God wants her, through the guidance of His Word, her own spiritual counsel, and the promptings of a godly husband.

—Mildred Meythaler

Appendix 2

Second-Class Citizenship
in the Kingdom of God

(from *Christianity Today*, 1971)

I'M TIRED OF being considered a second-class citizen in the Kingdom of God. I'm not considered that by God, of course, but by men. I'm not black. I am a woman. The church visible has in its life and ministry ignored to a frightening degree the truth of Galatians 3:28: "There is no such thing as Jew and Greek, slave and freeman, male and female; for you are all one person in Christ Jesus" (NEB).

Although early Christianity did help to liberate women from the degrading position of being considered chattel, the Christian Church has not been a leader in the struggle for *full* equality for women in society, nor has it allowed women to experience freedom from society's prejudices within the Church. Is it not true that Christ came not only to remove the barrier of sin between man and God but also to break down every wall separating one human being from another? But the wall between women's and men's participation in the life of the Church has never been broken down.

Even where the divisions between Christians of different races have been recognized as sinful and contrary to God's view of mankind, and where these divisions have been reduced to some degree, the old prejudices against women still exist. The pastor of a multi-racial church that has made real progress in overcoming racial divisions expressed surprise when he was asked about the progress his congregation had made in welcom-

179

ing women to full participation in church life. He had not even identified the prejudices against women in the church as an area of concern, nor had his wife.

Sermons, books, and "talks" on women in the Bible or in the Church are usually focused on the idea that women can be effective helpers to men who are seeking to follow God. The theme is that even women can be worthy servants of God if they will be submissive (to men), exert their influence indirectly, and above all remember their place. That place is seen as somehow very different from, and inferior to, men's place in the church. Women must inquire of men what place they have designated for women, and this will usually be the kitchen or nursery, not the room where the board of elders meets. Did not our Lord specifically commend Mary for sitting at his feet, that is, for learning directly from him, instead of fulfilling the conventional woman's role of preparing meals? How many women have missed out on opportunities for spiritual and intellectual growth by being in the kitchen or the nursery, areas rarely staffed by men?

The Church has long invited women to become members, to work in the Sunday school, and to serve refreshments to any and all groups. Their role in the church has been preparing and serving fellowship meals, assisting with the music (but not leading the singing!), preparing missionary outfits, and tending the nursery—all activities that could just as well and perhaps better be carried on as a cooperative effort by men and women. Where are the men now elected to wait at table as in Acts 6:2,3? Women's groups have in every sense been auxiliary, not necessarily to the Lord's work but to the activities of the men who make all decisions in the Church and hold most or all of the important offices.

If we are to judge by the composition of boards and committees in the average church, many pastors and laymen must agree with the pastor who is reported to have said that there are few offices in the church that a woman can hold. Why? Is it that they take more seriously the Apostle Paul's admonition about women keeping silent in church (how many elders speak in church anyway?) than his statement that in Christ there is no such thing as male and female?

Undoubtedly Paul's words have had a decisive impact on

the Church in its attitude toward women. Statements on the roles of men and women in marriage are cited very often in the Christian community, and it seems clear that Paul expected and commanded wives to be in subjection to their husbands in marriage (see Eph. 5:22–24, 33; Col. 3:18; Titus 2:5). But Paul's suggestions on another marital possibility, celibacy (see First Corinthians 7), are not taken seriously by very many Protestants, perhaps because of a reaction to Catholic practice. Moreover, the instructions Paul gives on the wife's role are often associated in the evangelical's mind with the Apostle's suggestions concerning the role of women in the Church. But his comparison of the relation of wife to husband with that of the Church to Christ (Eph. 5:22–24) cannot be translated into the affirmation that women in the Church are to be submissive to men in the Church; it means, obviously, that women and men in the Church are to be obedient to Christ. The relation of the female to the male in marriage is compared with the relation of human beings of both sexes to Christ.

In Paul's most explicit instructions concerning women's role in the Church, his preference, very likely conditioned by the society around about him, is expressed as his personal wish rather than as a dogmatic prescription for church practice. As in his treatment of celibacy ("I have no instructions from the Lord, but I give my judgment as one who by God's mercy is fit to be trusted" I Cor. 7:25, NEB), Paul's preferences in church life—that men should offer the prayers, that women should be learners, not teachers, and that women should be quiet and not domineer over men—are introduced with the phrases "It is my desire . . . " and "I do not permit . . . " (I Tim. 2:8–12), revealing a personal bias in his instructions.

It is understandable that Paul's command concerning bishops that immediately follows should be expressed in masculine terms (I Tim. 3:1–7). The statement on the sex of deacons does not appear to be so clearly in favor of men only; a note in the New English Bible includes the word *deaconesses* also (verse 11).

One clear indication that Paul himself did not follow completely his own policy statements on women in the Church is found in Romans 16:1. The first person mentioned in this section of many names is "Phoebe, a fellow-Christian who holds office in the congregation at Cenchreae." And Paul requests of the Roman Christians: "Give her, in the fellowship of the Lord, a welcome worthy of God's people, and stand by her in any business in which she may need your help for she has herself been a good friend to many, including myself" (Rom. 16:2). Mentioned by Paul in another letter are women "who shared my struggles in the cause of the Gospel" (Phil. 4:3). That fewer women than men are mentioned in the epistles as fellow laborers and church officials very likely indicates that the early Church was influenced by the societal pattern of male dominance.

And how are we to deal with First Corinthians 11:5, which indicates that women do pray and prophesy, since directions are given for the covering of their heads while they are engaged in these activities? In the same chapter we read: "In Christ's fellowship woman is as essential to man as man to woman. If woman was made out of man, it is through woman that man now comes to be; and God is the source of all" (I Cor. 11:11, 12, NEB). Of course, many women, long trained to be silent in church affairs or to make their influence felt through their husbands, are very reluctant to put themselves forward in seeking church offices, and a great deal of potential of God is being wasted.

What I propose is that the Christian community examine *all* the Scriptures dealing with women's role in the Church and that it prayerfully consider the possibility that spiritually mature and capable women should be called upon as often as men possessing these qualities to provide leadership in the Church by serving on governing and policy-making boards.

The prejudices against women in the Church carry over into other religious organizations. The president of a large evangelical organization working with students, wanting to encourage me, revealed his belief that women faculty members *can* have an effective ministry on the campus, too—as if being a woman is somehow a stigma that prevents one from bearing witness to Christ's transforming love in the same way that a man might. It is no surprise that this same organization offers a faculty handbook in which one chapter is entitled "The Faculty Member's Wife and Home." Faculty "member" means faculty *man*, apparently.

The small number of women on boards of major denominations shows clearly that although women make up an important segment of the membership and work force of the Church, they are not in positions of leadership generally. One notable exception was the election of Cynthia Wedel as president of the National Council of Churches (something that would probably never happen in the National Association of Evangelicals). Of course, when pressed, some people would admit they preferred a woman to a black, which seemed to be the case with the election of Mrs. Wedel. I asked the missionary-personnel secretary of one denomination whether her church gave equal status to women, and she replied that the few women officers of the church were not paid commensurate with their training or on the same salary scale as the men on the staff.

The Christian Church, in its selective application of the Apostle Paul's statements, has not been revealing to the world the truth of Galatians 3:28 that in Christ there is no distinction between male and female. It is time for the body of believers to do all things possible to show that humankind's sinful divisions do not apply in the Church. Certainly heaven will not be segregated according to sex any more than by color. If we truly believe that Christ's redemption delivers us from seeing people in categories, from stereotyping them from birth according to color, sex and other differences, then let us, as members of the Christian Church and of Christ's body, begin to be a witness to the fact that Christ does indeed liberate us— all of us, women and men, black and white—to be what *he* wants us to be, and not what our sin-racked culture with all its prejudices wishes to make of us by squeezing us into its mold.

—Ruth A. Schmidt

Appendix 3

Consciousness-Raising
in the Church

AFTER READING *All We're Meant to Be*, I began wondering how to share my new insights about "biblical feminism" with others. Soon, with optimism and energy I moved into action at the large evangelical church to which I belonged. My first step was to lead my own adult Sunday school class in an examination of women's roles at our church. I announced three sessions: first, we would discuss what women's roles were; then, what they should be; and finally, how to change them. During the opening class I passed out questionnaires to discover people's opinions on what women's roles at our church were and should be, and we discussed those questions. I was surprised to see a couple of board members and older people from other classes attending my class; they made sure that the doctrine of women not ruling men was heard. I shared the research I had done—that 62 percent of the 1,700 members of our church were women; that men held 27 out of 30 positions on the ruling council; that all five pastors and most other official leaders were men. In class discussion we agreed that women predominated in preschool and elementary Sunday school teaching, in clerical work, and in kitchen jobs, but we disagreed on whether this division of labor constituted a problem.

For the second class of the series, I asked four leading women—a church secretary, a pastor's wife, a woman elder, and an active woman—to talk about their experiences as women at our church. As it turned out, the one most opposed to equality for women (who had said she couldn't talk for five minutes) talked for half an hour. In the few minutes left to her after the other speakers had aired their views, the speaker nearest to being a feminist said almost nothing. Apparently she could not bring herself to tell in public the woeful tale of obstruction of energetic women she had told me in private.

In our final session we never got to the last step: how to change things. Nonetheless, undaunted, I compiled the questionnaires, speeches, and class discussion, and wrote a report containing these results and eleven specific suggestions on how to begin improving opportunities for women. I sent about ten copies of my letter to the pastors and other church leaders. After not receiving any answer for two months, I finally went to see the head pastor and to present my list of suggestions for women at our church. He was friendly but pointed out that he could not take a position from the pulpit. It was his job to mediate among the various interest groups at the church. And as to inviting women preachers rather frequently or hiring a woman for the next pastoral vacancy, those were nice ideas; he would do what he could, but of course his power was limited.

Satisfied that I had made a good start on changing women's roles at my church, I settled back into other activities until an announcement one Sunday jolted me: fifteen people had been nominated for ten positions on the church's ruling council in the annual elections—twelve men and three women. I was appalled. That was no better than the current ratio of men to women; in fact, fewer women were running than had run the previous year. I began working to get a few more women nominated from the floor. I found that many of the leading women had been asked to run, but had refused for various reasons. Some felt that women should not be council members; others were too busy with children and families (though their husbands had had time to serve on the council). Others were afraid of being the only assertive woman in the men's club of council members. Others—including the talented president of the large, active women's group—simply felt inadequate. "Oh no," she said, "I don't know anything. I couldn't be on the ruling council with all those businessmen." Others told me that women under sixty could not get elected, especially women who might actually speak up in meetings. The few women already on the council tended to regard the office as an honorary reward for years of service—not a place for them to speak and take positions. Every woman had an excuse. I spent one whole day talking and praying with a woman who I hoped would run from the floor, but she finally backed out.

When election night came, two friends and I went to the meeting with a feeling of defeat. We almost nominated ourselves, but decided that that might anger people and hurt the chances of electing women candidates in the future. Instead, I got up during the election meeting, pointed out the imbalance between men and women candidates, and made an impassioned plea for prayer and work to change the balance in the next election.

The positive response from people who had heard me was encouraging. They all said, "Next year!" We agreed that a warm, supportive group was needed, where potential women board members could discuss things holding them back, encourage each other, plan a strategy to elect several women together, and provide on-going support for those elected. This group would be an official subcommittee of a standing committee. When fall came, I put announcements in the church bulletin for the first meeting of the women's committee and made a blue folder for my files marked "Women's Movement at Church." Three of us were present for the first monthly meeting; three for the second; and, for the third meeting, just my best friend and I. In discouragement, we disbanded.

Meanwhile, I led other adult education classes on women's roles in the church. The associate pastor and I taught one series together; he had become a supportive friend. Studying the issue of women in the church, he eventually preached a sermon urging broader roles for women. One Mother's Day I spoke to a class of older, married adults on "Faith of our Mothers" and was moved by feeling sisterhood with the women present and with women throughout church history. Other efforts included putting key books into the church library and setting up a special collection of books on women in the church. I tried to get the church's book sales room to offer Christian feminist books and the lectures given by the assistant pastor and myself. After a long struggle, the woman in charge finally permitted the suspect materials into her bookroom.

All these efforts were usually greeted with a chuckle or a tolerant smile. Occasionally there was hostility. The goals that I considered so elementary—such as having half the council members be women—were seen as radical.

Finally, my own consciousness became raised to a point where the male-dominated worship service grated on me. I would sit and look at the four male pastors up there in front of the church and at the laymen usually reading the Scriptures, and would find it hard to worship God. When I was served communion by twenty-five males, I would feel anger and be in no state to take communion. At the early service, there might be one or two women serving communion. Even when I gave my offering, male ushers collected it—and the money went to pay a staff that was top-heavy with males. Women on the church staff were at the bottom, and underpaid.

About that time I learned that only one woman was going to be nominated in the upcoming election of church council members. Quite a few had turned down the nomination, as in the previous year. The news forced me into a serious reevaluation of God's will for me at my church. I had been offered the nomination but had refused it, thinking that my role was to work behind the scenes for the talented, middle-aged women who should be elders, as well as work for the Evangelical Women's Caucus. Should I, at age twenty-seven, be an "elder" on the council of my church and invest most of my time and energy there if elected? My efforts thus far seemed to be swallowed up like pebbles thrown into a lake. The more I thought about it, time and the working of the Holy Spirit seemed to be the only solutions for my church. Perhaps in twenty years . . .

With my new perspective, I questioned the worth of even continuing to be a member there. It often took me a whole week of "quiet times" to dissolve my hurt and hard feelings from one Sunday morning. One day when I went to church confident of being able to love whomever I met, I saw a "Successful Fulfilled Womanhood Seminar" poster and flyers prominently displayed next to the pastor's door (from a Bill

Gothard-related group devoted to teaching submission to wives). I flew into a rage.

I decided to leave that church for two reasons: my spiritual health and the health of the Christian church. I needed a place where I could worship and gain strength in my walk with the Lord. And the Christian church needed to have support withdrawn from any lukewarm church that was afraid to proclaim the Good News to women.

It took me nine months to find a church reasonably in line with God's will for women. Unfortunately, this church is not evangelical. But it is solidly Christian and it is a warm, loving family, where women preach about once a month and participate rather fully in all levels of service. I wrote a letter to all the leaders of my old church, explaining my reason for leaving and saying "The Lord will have to watch over me until the evangelical churches become a more faithful witness to the liberating power of the Holy Spirit."

In the meantime, the church has hired yet another male pastor, the sixth, this time for junior high children.

Appendix 4

The Evangelical
Women's Caucus

FEMINISM IS DEFINED in Webster's Dictionary as ". . . the principle that women should have political, economic, and social rights equal to those of men." The Evangelical Women's Caucus is a national organization, with grass-roots chapters, that seeks to unite evangelical feminists in the United States and Canada. The EWC welcomes anyone who considers herself, or himself, both evangelical and feminist—that is, committed to a personal relationship with Jesus Christ as Savior and Lord, to the authority of the Bible as the inspired word of God, and to equal rights for women and men in society, church, and home.

The Evangelical Women's Caucus was formed in 1974 in Chicago at the second Thanksgiving Workshop of Evangelicals for Social Action. It was one implementation of that group's 1973 Chicago Declaration which had stated in part: "We acknowledge that we have encouraged men to prideful domination and women to irresponsible passivity. So we call both men and women to mutual submission and active discipleship." The EWC is committed to enabling women to identify, develop, and use responsibly their gifts for the furtherance of God's Kingdom, without regard to sex-role stereotypes. "We are committed to moving the church toward greater openness to the ministry of women in the church and in the world. We strive for love and justice as both sexes learn to serve one another."

189

The first major event of the Evangelical Women's Caucus was a national conference on "Women in Transition: A Biblical Approach to Feminism," held over Thanksgiving weekend 1975 in Washington, D.C. More than 360 women and men from 36 states and from Canada attended. They represented a wide spectrum of the Christian church: mainline Protestants, Mennonites, representatives of the holiness tradition, Pentecostals and charismatics, and a few Roman Catholics.

Members of a temporary national steering committee led in the founding of local EWC chapters in Los Angeles, Washington, D.C., Albany, N.Y., Minneapolis, San Francisco Bay Area, Detroit, Newark, and Boston. Evon Bachaus of Minneapolis served as national coordinator for one year. Early actions included developing a network and directory of Christian feminists, publishing a national newsletter, compiling informational packets, consciousness-raising in local churches, and holding local and regional conferences.

A second national conference, "Women and the Ministries of Christ," was held in Pasadena, California, in June 1978, sponsored by the Southwestern Chapter of the Evangelical Women's Caucus and Fuller Theological Seminary. About 900 women and men took part in plenary sessions, Bible discussions, study groups, and workshops (95 options!). A national organizational meeting at the end of the conference approved a statement of faith and bylaws for incorporation as a nonprofit organization. These documents can be obtained by sending a stamped, self-addressed legal-size envelope to the national EWC office (P.O. Box 64582, Los Angeles, CA 90064). National dues are $10 yearly for regular members; $5 for students and low-income persons. A national newsletter is included in membership.

A small journal/newsletter of biblical feminism, *Daughters of Sarah* (Reta Finger, editorial coordinator), is published six times yearly. Address: 4011 N. Avers, Chicago, IL 60618 ($3.00; Canada $4.00).

A second biblical feminist publication, a bi-monthly magazine born in 1978, is *freeindeed* (Diane R. Jepsen and Jan Abramsen, editors). Address: 262 E. Union Blvd., Bethlehem, PA 18018 ($8.00; Canada $9.50).

The first thesis on the Evangelical Women's Caucus and its

antecedents, "Feminists in the American Evangelical Movement," was written at Pacific School of Religion, Berkeley, CA, by Ina J. Kau, 1977. Another thesis, "From Hierarchy to Equality: A Comparison of Past and Present Interpretations of 1 Cor. 11:2–16 in Relation to the Changing Status of Women in Society," written by Linda Mercadante at Regent College, "has brought to light many fresh possibilities that illumine the apostle Paul's feminism without diminishing his authority" (Clark Pinnock). Available from the writer, c/o Regent College, 2130 Wesbrook Mall, Vancouver, B.C. V6T 1W6 ($6.50).